WOULD YOU BELIEVE?

BOOKS BY TOM HARPUR

Harpur's Heaven and Hell (1983)
For Christ's Sake (1986; reissued 1993)
Always on Sunday (1988)
Life After Death (1991)
God Help Us (1992)
The Uncommon Touch (1994)
Would You Believe? (1996)

Would You Believe?

Finding God Without Losing Your Mind

Tom Harpur

M&S

Canadian Cataloguing in Publication Data

Harpur, Tom
    Would you believe? : finding God without losing
your mind

ISBN 0-7710-3947-6

1. God.   2. Faith.   I. Title.

BT102.H37 1996   231'.042   C95-933331-2

The publishers acknowledge the support of the Canada
Council and the Ontario Arts Council for their
publishing program.

Typesetting by M&S, Toronto

Printed and bound in Canada
The paper used in this book is acid-free

McClelland & Stewart Inc.
The Canadian Publishers
481 University Avenue
Toronto, Ontario
M5G 2E9

1 2 3 4 5   00 99 98 97 96

For Elizabeth, Margaret and Mary Catharine

Contents

Acknowledgements

Much is owed to many people in the writing and publication of any book. I cannot mention all those whose thinking and encouragement have resulted in this volume, but I would like to single out a few whose contribution was crucial. I want particularly to thank my two tutors at Oriel College, Oxford, who long ago first challenged me to think for myself. Richard Robinson, my philosophy don, was a compassionate atheist, who taught me the importance of holding a reasonable faith. Professor Ronald Brunt, who was my Greek and Roman history tutor, taught me the enormous difference between opinion and evidence. I am grateful also to Douglas Fisher of London, Ontario, who heads the North American Spiritual-Cultural Development Satellite Network. He was the first to introduce me both to the person and then to the writing of Fr. Thomas Berry, cultural historian and "ecologian" par excellence. He also was the one who brought Dr. R. M. Bucke's seminal book, *Cosmic Consciousness*, to my attention (see Chapter 5). Once again, the readers of my syndicated column in the *Sunday Star* have incurred my indebtedness as well. Their enthusiastic response to my request for assistance in researching blocks to faith in our time resulted in the framework for chapters 3 and 4. I know that Susan, my wife and collaborator in all my endeavours, requires no accolades, but I would be remiss if I didn't once more express my thanks for her unflagging support, her shrewd editorial comments, and her essential help in getting the manuscript into its final shape. Last, but by no means least, to all the staff at McClelland & Stewart, and particularly to publisher Doug Gibson and my faithful and tireless editor, Dinah Forbes, my warmest appreciation.

"The old order changeth, yielding place to new;
And God fulfils himself in many ways."

Alfred, Lord Tennyson, "The Passing of Arthur,"
Idylls of the King

"The heart has its reasons which reason knows nothing of."

Blaise Pascal, *Pensées.*

"The challenge that faces humanity is unique, for it has never occurred before. Clearly a new kind of creative surge is needed to meet it. This has to include not just a new way of doing science but a new approach to society, and even more, a new kind of consciousness."

Physicist David Bohm in
Science, Order, and Creativity, by David Bohm and
F. David Peat. (Toronto: Bantam Books, 1987).

Introduction

♀

Lenny Bruce, the American comedian, once quipped, "Every day, people are straying away from the church and going back to God." There is considerable truth in this seemingly paradoxical remark. There is a vast spiritual search going on at the moment, not just in North America but all around the globe, and there are signs of it everywhere. Consider the best-seller lists in the *New York Times* and elsewhere and you will see that major books on spirituality not only top the non-fiction lists, but many of them stay there for months or even years. For example, Scott Peck's *The Road Less Travelled* has been a best-seller for over ten years. Conferences are now being held on spirituality and the business world. Even the World Bank held its first conference on ethics, spirituality and development in New York in the fall of 1995. There is, on the one hand, a kind of wistful nostalgia for the faith of one's childhood or of one's heritage. Yet, at the same time, there is also a widespread, intuitive sense that it is impossible to pretend that nothing has changed the nature of these beliefs. For the majority, simply going back to what was good for our parents or forebears is no solution at all. People want and need a faith that makes sense in the world of today. Above all, they do not want to purchase faith at the expense of numbing, denying or offending their intellect. They must either have a God whom they can love with all their mind and intelligence or they can have no God at all.

The question we face is: Is it possible, given all the shaking of the foundations of religion that has gone on in this century, combined with an incredible explosion of information, for us to find and hold a living faith in God, one that is convincing in the present age? How would one go about this, and what kind of God is there to be found? How are we to deal with the vexing problems and doubts that come up as soon as these matters are raised? In other words, how, in today's world, can we find faith in God without losing our minds? These are the issues tackled in *Would You Believe?* There are few, if any, that are more important for one's life.

This is not a book about reasons for going or returning to church, temple, or synagogue, even though some readers may be moved to do so after considering what it has to say. Nor does it try to make converts to any particular religion or creed, as belonging to an organized religion and finding spiritual reality are not necessarily the same thing.

Nevertheless, part of the angst surrounding the present spiritual search comes from the fact that there are numerous siren voices without, and sometimes within, suggesting that a return to "the old-time religion" might be both possible and desirable after all. Certainly that is the message of the fundamentalist or ultra-conservative factions in all faiths today. Because of their high profile in the media, especially television, in North America and elsewhere, and their apparent successes at a time when many other religious institutions seem to be fading fast, they give the impression that in order to find faith one has to embrace their particular version of belief or nothing at all. Still, for many people today who are perhaps attracted by the fundamentalists' energy and promise of certainty and yet repelled by their glibness, their oversimplifications and their implicit intolerances, the intellectual price of such a route to faith seems simply too high. So, an anxious impasse is reached. One wants to believe, but the options appear too narrow and the intellectual obstacles in the way seem insurmountable.

I describe myself as "an uncomfortable Christian." By this I mean something akin to what Robert Frost had in mind when he wrote: "I have a lover's quarrel with the world." My "lover's quarrel" is with traditional or orthodox Christianity. In other words, while I owe much to the Christian tradition and will always be grateful for having been nurtured in it, I am now keenly aware of many aspects that are no longer "comfortable" or acceptable in that tradition on intellectual or moral grounds. My greatest unease (and it applies to any other religion making similar assertions) is with all Christian claims to exclusivity – the view that there is only one true way or that outside the Church there is no, or only a very limited, salvation. It follows therefore that I am not concerned here to put forth a case for some form of "churchianity." There are plenty of other books today on that theme. What follows is meant for that great and growing company of people everywhere in the Western world who have drifted away from the religion of their parents or who have lost faith entirely and who, recognizing the spiritual vacuum at the core of their being, now long for something more.

Here I caution those who are already committed to some traditional approach to religion and find that it entirely meets their spiritual needs and aspirations. They could be disturbed by this exploration. This is not a book intended for those who are happily "at ease in Zion."

I would also like to say why I have chosen to begin with the chapters setting out why I believe and what I believe. You could argue that they properly belong to the end of such a discussion. However, on issues as large and as crucial as these, I am determined to be as honest and "up front" as possible with you, the reader. There is , as T. S. Eliot reminds us, a profound identity and linkage between the beginning and the end of any truly significant journey. In the journey before us, chapters 1 and 2 hold the *raison d'être* of all the rest.

What ensues here, then, is one man's wrestlings with some universal questions. I don't begin to claim that the answers I propose or the suggestions I make are at all infallible. They do, however, come out of an honest, though obviously quite imperfect, lived encounter with the Ultimate Reality they struggle to describe. May that same Presence be with you as you read.

Note: God is beyond gender, transcending all human sexuality. But, while I am aware that the traditional use of the male pronoun in referring to God certainly needs to be challenged, I intend to follow it here. Such contrivances as he/she when referring to the Deity can be clumsy and obtrude unnecessarily into the flow of the text. However, my use of he, him, or his in this book should in no way be taken as evidence of assent to patriarchal or sexist views on the part of the author. I use them only because they are the most convenient and readily understood of any terminology available.

One last matter: On the few occasions when the Bible is quoted, the text is that of the King James Version (KJV) unless otherwise indicated. The New Revised Standard Version (NRSV) is more accurate but less familiar to most people.

I

Why I Believe

Most people in this country and elsewhere, when asked about the subject by pollsters or others, say they believe in God. They may go on to qualify this in various ways by saying "there's got to be something behind all this" or by talking about a cosmic mind, a first cause, or a similar reality. But, surveys of all descriptions in North America, for example – ever since polling began – reveal that the majority believe that they believe in God.

If the majority believe, why then, one may well ask, is there any need to write this book? Well, there is a need because there are a couple of problems with this answer. First there is the problem of why the majority respond this way. Saying "I believe in God" is an unthinking reflex for many people, almost a cultural necessity, especially in North America. For others it's a superstitious avoidance of risking bad luck – a sort of insurance clause in case some things they learned in childhood might just happen to have a core of truth. They'd rather not offend any deity, in case there happens to be one! Second, there is a problem in the content of the reply itself. You can say you believe in God in a general, vague way that is completely divorced from any personal experience or commitment. You may give the idea of there being a God some quick intellectual assent but have never thought much more about it. Or, as is the case with most people who are genuinely seeking to grow spiritually today, you can say you believe in God while remaining totally confused about the kind of God you believe in and about what a living faith would entail or feel like if you had it. In other words, you could conceivably take a poll in which all those asked said they believe in God, and still have an acute crisis of faith. The situation is rather like that of the man in the Gospels who cried out: "Lord, I believe: help Thou my unbelief!"

Before I go any further, I should stress that when I talk about faith, I am decidedly not talking about *blind* faith. I remember how even as a choirboy, complete with high starched collar and white surplice, I would sit in the chancel of St. Saviour's Anglican Church, in Toronto's east end, and carry on a mental debate with the sermon, the lessons or the hymns. As rational beings, we must have reasons for our beliefs. While any God worthy of the name is by definition far beyond reason's total grasp, nevertheless a faith that will not stand rational scrutiny, that contradicts reason in any fundamental way, is not a faith for human beings. True spiritual belief is never "blind."

Let me be clear on this point. I have no difficulty, as you will see, with aspects of faith and belief that go beyond reason – that are what I call non-rational. To quote Pascal, "The heart has its reasons which reason knows nothing of." But, the kind of belief we are concerned with here can never be irrational. Standing in the Judeo-Christian tradition as I do, I have always been deeply conscious of the biblical command to love God with all one's mind, as well as with one's heart and strength. The Anglican Church, in which I was raised and later ordained, with all its many faults and weaknesses, to its credit has from the very outset insisted upon the central importance of a faith that is reasonable and firmly based upon sound scholarship and learning. I have myself always felt closest to that group of Anglicans who flourished at Cambridge University between 1633 and 1688, known as the Cambridge Platonists. They stood between the Puritans on the one hand and the High Anglicans on the other. They called for tolerance and comprehension based upon their view that reason was the final arbiter of both natural and revealed religion. Taking an almost mystical view of reason, they described it as "the candle of the Lord."

Why, then, do I believe in God? Put as simply as possible, I do so because quite literally, to quote Martin Luther from another context, "I can do no other." This does not mean that belief and faith come easily to me, that I have no doubts, or that I am a believer by constitution, temperament or from lack of exposure to the arguments and criticisms of atheists, agnostics or others. Most readers of my books and columns over the years are acquainted with the sceptical bent of my mind and of my deep respect for evidence. Like my New Testament namesake, Thomas, I ask for solid ground upon which to build any edifice of trust. However, the best way I can explain why I believe is to say that in the end I find myself compelled to believe. It's a compulsion that flows from the head and also from the heart. It comes from both aspects of the brain, the logical and the intuitive. Indeed, it's ultimately an affair of body, mind and spirit. After years of study, of travels around the world, of rich experience in several callings, I must confess: nothing else makes as much sense to me.

"This cannot be an accident!" That's how the late Gordon Sinclair, the radio and television personality – whose attacks on organized religion were well known – once replied when I asked him how he felt on looking up at night and seeing the vast panoply of stars above his Muskoka cottage. "There are galaxies beyond galaxies beyond galaxies," he said. "At that point, I must believe in God." This admission, made during an interview for a television program I once hosted, called "Paradox," surprised many viewers at the time because of Sinclair's notoriously loud, public professions of agnosticism over the years. He went on to say he agreed that there must be "some kind of divine purpose" in and behind the universe but that he could not accept a God who intervenes in human affairs. Asked whether his idea of God was that of one who is "somehow then outside, dispassionately watching everything," he replied: "I don't know."

We will come back to the concepts of an interventionist or non-interventionist God later. For now, my reason for citing Sinclair is to show that even a professional agnostic such as he, faced with the splendour, the harmony, the mysteries, and the immense reaches of the natural world, found it difficult, even impossible, to speak in terms of accident, chance, or the rolling of cosmic dice. The same is true for me. As I experience the miracle of life and the wonders of our universe, my certainty that it is grounded in and sustained by an intelligent, transcendent-yet-immanent personal energy whom we call God increases daily. (Does this raise intellectual problems? Yes, of course, and we'll discuss them in due time.)

The first question to ask about our universe is: Why is there anything here at all? Why are there galaxies, stars and planets? Why on earth are there continents and oceans, mountains and running streams? Why has life evolved to a point where, uniquely in the human brain and consciousness, it can contemplate and celebrate itself? What is the ultimate explanation for the ingenuity of the human immune system or for the beauty and power of great art, music, literature or drama? How is it that some scientists today are speaking of an anthropic principle – that the universe itself seems to have been prepared for us, to have been designed with self-aware beings in mind? It has always seemed to me to require infinitely more faith to believe that everything from the genius of Mozart to the mysterious beauty of a newborn baby or from the glittering array of stars in the heavens to the glory of a fall day in a forest of maples is the result of a purely random series of mindless, purposeless events which mean nothing and are ultimately going nowhere. The statistical odds against the chance meeting of all the various conditions necessary for the emergence and nurture of intelligent life on our planet alone are overwhelming.

What I find interesting in this respect is that more and more physicists and other scientists today are coming to this position. While it would be foolish to claim, as some unthinking religionists do, that the majority of scientists now accept a more or less orthodox concept of God, nevertheless the growing consensus over the necessity for some kind of "God hypothesis" is a startling development. One of the leading exponents of this viewpoint is the eminent mathematician and philosopher from Australia, Paul Davies, who won the coveted Templeton Prize in Religion in 1995 for his work in bringing science and religion together. In his 1992 book, *The Mind of God*, Davies writes: "I cannot believe that our existence in this universe is a mere quirk of fate, an accident of history, an incidental blip in the great cosmic drama. Our involvement is too intimate. . . . We are truly meant to be here." That, though in a slightly less sophisticated way, is precisely what the agnostic Gordon Sinclair was also compelled to say. Obviously, it is my deepest conviction as well.

But, there is more than what is called "the argument from design" behind my reasons for believing. There is also the "argument from within." There is more than one way of knowing. There is the way of the intellect and reason, and there is the more immediate and spontaneous, intuitive knowing of the heart or soul. True, logicians in the past – and particularly at Oxford during my undergraduate days in the early 1950s, when the positivist philosopher Gilbert Ryle held sway – have maintained that only empirical evidence (evidence gained through the five senses and able to be tested and verified) leads to real knowledge. The technical name for this approach is Logical Positivism. But, this approach to knowing, which effectively ignored all metaphysical or spiritual reality, has thankfully been largely abandoned today. We need to be reminded that most of the things we would be prepared to die for cannot be directly known empirically or be "proved" by scientific experiments. If you ask happily married men or women whether they know their spouse loves them, they will quickly and confidently say yes. How do they know? They just do. It's not a knowledge that contradicts what they know in their minds, but it flows chiefly from their hearts. The senses play a part in this knowing but they are not all of it. We could say the same about beauty, friendship or the knowledge of right and wrong.

At this level of knowing, my whole being knows and is aware of a numinous Presence both without, pervading the universe, and within. This knowledge doesn't spring from any kind of mystical experience. Although I have read much about them and, as a journalist, have interviewed many people who have had them, I am not myself given to seeing visions, apparitions, hearing external voices, or other such paranormal phenomena. I believe they occur; I just don't have them or at least have not done so to date. Nevertheless, the conviction that we are not alone in the universe, that we are made by, watched over, responsible to, and finally destined for God has remained a constant throughout my life even at the worst moments of emptiness, pain and dark doubts. This, let me make perfectly clear, is in no way a claim to some special, invisible pipeline or connection to God. It's a perfectly natural, common-sense, gut knowledge that we are spiritual beings created for fellowship with the Spirit-intelligence we know and describe as God. As the Psalmist said centuries ago: "Deep calleth unto deep." There is something in all of us that intuits and seeks after a divine Presence which already is seeking us. It is portrayed in Jesus' parable of the prodigal son: When the profligate "came to himself" and started home, he found his father was already out on the road coming to meet him.

Like many of you, I experience a renewal of this

intuitive awareness of God most particularly when I am alone – or with kindred spirits – in the country-side. Back when I was the minister of a suburban parish east of Toronto, I used to be very sceptical of those who insisted they didn't need to go to church because they "felt closer to God" in their garden, out hiking or golfing. It seemed like an excuse for not attending or supporting the church, and I had doubts whether any of these "blue domers," as we called them then, ever actually gave God a thought while out on the golf green or on a beach. Nevertheless, when I am honest with myself, I have to admit that I have only rarely felt in church the kind of peace and deep harmony with my own being as well as the cosmos itself that I have nearly always felt while hiking by a purling stream, sitting by the ocean watching a sunset, cross-country skiing through snow-laden woods, or watching leaves silently twist and fall in early October beside a northern lake.

This is not to disparage formal worship in a church, temple or synagogue. We will come to a fuller discussion of that shortly. It's simply to acknowledge the truth of what the ecologian (as he calls himself) Fr. Thomas Berry is saying when he writes that nature itself is "the first book of revelation" because it came into existence billions of years before the lessons of the Bible and other sacred texts were thought of, let alone written down. The lake beside which I live and write is a kettle lake formed at the end of the last Ice Age, some twelve thousand years ago, by the melting of the ice cap. The fact that it is older than any of the great world religions helps give me a perspective only nature can bring. Creation's great beauty and astounding mysteries speak to the intellect, as we have seen. But, like millions of others down the ages, I am also aware there is a Presence pervading and communicating through it that addresses us at a more profound level once we are sensitive to it.

There is more. This Presence, which confronts us in and through the mountains, the flowers, the birds, animals, fish and all the rest of the natural world, also meets us in other people. In our coming together in friendship, in family, in service or in other intimate relationships, we are sometimes aware of a Third Element or Dimension. I will resist the temptation to cite a host of witnesses to this fact and simply tell you that, without being unduly mystical or imaginative, I have experienced moments – sometimes quite unexpected – in being with or talking to others when, deep inside, I become aware of something or Someone far greater than the sum of the participants. I sense what I can only describe as a weightiness and a shining depth to the interchange of feelings and ideas that give them a significance far beyond their surface value. Suddenly I am aware of echoes or vibrations of Another Voice in what is said, or sometimes also unsaid, in the encounter. This is most real in the intimacies of a marriage where one truly loves and is loved. While orthodox Christians believe this kind of experience happens when "two or three are gathered together in my name," my own conviction – and experience – is that it happens all the time whether or not the people concerned are believers. If it is true that "in Him we live and move and have our being," then it only makes sense that any coming together of humans enhances the possibility of this reality breaking through to consciousness. In sum, there is much in a face-to-face meeting with other people that speaks to me of what some theologians have called "the Beyond in our midst" – God.

I have deliberately left the consideration of sacred books and texts – what theologians call divine revelation – until the close of this chapter. Partly, this is because I have to confess to being totally put off by religionists who wave a large Bible or other holy book and demand literal belief in its pages because it's "the Word of God." When asked why anyone should accept the proposition that this or that text is God's Word, they usually reply "because that's what it plainly claims to be." The circularity of this reasoning is absurd. Since all language about God, in sacred books or elsewhere, is human language, the product of human thought and reasoning, it is always inadequate, partial, and prone to misunderstanding and error. I do not now believe – and never have believed – in infallible books or infallible prelates, swamis or gurus of any rank or description.

The Bible, for example, is, for me, the single most inspiring book in the world. But for all that, it is a very human book, replete with factual and textual errors, as well as frequently coarse or primitive concepts of God and morality. Genocide, slavery and polygamy, as well as capital punishment for minor offenses, are among the things said to have been commanded or countenanced by the deity. To say you believe it "from cover to cover," as most conservative Christians do, is in my view to have committed intellectual and ethical suicide. There are similar difficulties in a literal approach to the Qur'an, or any other holy book.

This is not the place for a full discussion of the symbolic or metaphorical nature of much of the biblical picture of God and his dealings with the world. I just want to say that despite what I have just written about the fallibility of the Bible and other sacred texts of world religions I do believe in God in part because of the witness of the Bible and revelation in general. All great literature is divinely inspired. I sense that the Bible is more fully God-inspired than, say, the works of Shakespeare, only because of its subject matter. It is focused wholly upon the story of God's interaction with his creation, particularly with humankind.

In spite of some passages that are puzzling, boring, or even morally offensive or downright contradictory, the Bible speaks to me more powerfully than any other book. Like millions through the ages, I am aware while reading it of being addressed by the Source and Founder of my very being. The descriptions given, the moral challenges flung down, and the words of healing and comfort offered in it transcend anything else that I have read in a lifetime of study. I can honestly say that, though my approach is often critical, I deeply love the Bible, both Testaments, and that any faith I have has always been challenged, illumined and nourished by the words of its various writers. I find its central message authenticated by my own thoughts, feelings and experience of life. The God it presents overall is the God I have come to know, however imperfectly and weakly. Virtually every page has passages that merit years of meditation and lessons it would take more than one lifetime to learn. Virtually every page has thoughts to make your heart soar and your mind take fresh hope and courage. For example, "They that wait upon the Lord shall renew their strength; they shall mount up with wings as eagles; they shall run and not be weary; and they shall walk and not faint." Or, those often repeated words of Christ: "Be not afraid."

These, then, are some of the reasons why I believe.

2

What I Believe

I write this chapter with some trepidation as there is a stigma attached to daring to set out for others what one believes oneself. Critics sometimes view it as a form of egotism. However, I feel that honesty demands it here. It seems only fair that you know what I believe, and I have no intention of asking or urging you to believe exactly the same. One of my cardinal beliefs is that each of us must work earnestly to come to his or her own beliefs and then take full responsibility for them. We will have various guides or gurus on our journey but the warp and woof of our faith – or lack thereof – is woven by us and our experience alone. It has been rightly observed that "God has no grandchildren." You cannot inherit a living spirituality. Unless what we believe has been tested in our unique life, it is a bogus creed and ultimately impotent.

BELIEF IN GOD

I believe in God. That is such an innocent, easy statement to make. Yet, without explanation or interpretation, it's about as ambiguous a sentence as any four
words could possibly form. The huge question, of
course, is what is meant by the word "God." But,
before coming to that, it's important to clarify the "I
believe" part. To say you believe in God can mean
simply that you are convinced there is an ultimate
entity, being or reality to which the name "God" is
normally given. But what I'm talking about here is
much more than a purely intellectual exercise. For
anyone serious about spiritual truth, saying "I
believe" is not just a matter of assenting to a proposition (such as, There is a God) but of full trust, commitment and intended obedience to him. A very
great deal is at stake, no less than one's life. Faith in
God always means a personal trust and confidence.

Now comes the truly hard part. The word "God"
– like the word "love" – has been used so loosely for
so long that it has become in many contexts almost meaningless. There is a lot to be said for the
Orthodox Jew's reluctance to speak or write God's
name in full at any time lest it be cheapened or
made common. The careless use of God's name,
which can empty it of all meaningful content,
though, is not the only risk. The other, even greater
risk is of equating God with a fixed image, definition
or creedal formula. The reason the Hebrew Bible

rails against idols so frequently is that all attempts to "pin God down," as it were, or to describe his being and nature with too great precision, lead to idolatry. Held too rigidly, our definitions or our ideas become, in their imperfection, a block to a genuine encounter. To avoid this, all thinking and speech about God has to be tentative, partial and openended. This was not, of course, the understanding of most of those who drew up the various statements of religious beliefs in the past. As a result, there is widespread idolatry today both within religious institutions, Christian and other, and without. Any fixed, closed, rigid, unexamined concept of deity is inevitably an idol. It is the God beyond all our fixed ideas who is truly God as he knows himself to be. The most realistic prayer of all is the one that begins: "Lord, we pray to you not as we know or think you are but as you know yourself to be. . . ."

THE "PERSONHOOD" OF GOD

While I have trouble with many of the orthodox statements about God, I am in accord with the ancient teaching found in most religions, and most particularly in the Judeo-Christian tradition, that God is a personal being. However, to be frank, many today who tell the pollsters they believe in God do not share this belief in God's personhood. They think instead of an impersonal "force" à la *Star Wars* or of some intelligent yet vague kind of First Mover and Creator that now stands aloof from the cosmos. This concept is very like the late-seventeenth- and early-eighteenth-century Deists' "clock-maker" model. Once started, the entire process supposedly runs by itself without any further intervention. This convenient "God of the philosophers" is not what I'm talking about here.

Nor am I talking about some imagined projection into the heavens of a very humanlike person who is simply much larger-than-life than mere mortals and endowed with all kinds of "super" powers such as omnipotence, omniscience and so on. This kind of anthropomorphism or making God in our own human image has gone on uncritically in much religious thought in the past and no doubt still today attends a lot of thinking on the subject. It should be pointed out clearly that a good deal of the biblical text, if taken literally, reinforces such a gross misconception.

C. S. Lewis, in his essay "Beyond Personality," comes closest to what I mean when I write about God's personhood. He argues that just as each stage of creation includes and goes beyond the previous stage – for example, plants consist of minerals and other inorganic elements but are living organisms; animals incorporate both inanimate and living features, including intelligence; and humans, comprising all of these, transcend them through the ability to be self-reflective – so too with God. His beingness, so to speak, both includes and transcends the human gift of personhood. Of course, Lewis's analogy, like all analogies, is not perfect. He did not intend, nor do I, to imply that God is a kind of higher evolution from humans. The point is that God exists not as some kind of cosmic gas or gravity-like energy but as an infinitely vast centre and field of energy and consciousness with a personal life that is "beyond personality." God includes what we think of as personhood yet transcends it. In his essence and deep unity, his personality is defined and moved by infinite compassion or love.

How do I know this? First, there is the extraordinary witness of the Bible and of the world's other sacred texts – where constantly, in and behind the literal text, God addresses humans in personal terms and accents – and, second, there is also the testimony of countless saints and sages over the centuries. The witness in literature, poetry, art and music is virtually endless. Most convincing of all to me is my own experience, which has confirmed for me what scripture and this rich tradition of the faithful has claimed. By reason and by intuition, through nature and by all the other means, God has always spoken to my soul in a manner I can only describe ultimately as personal. Like many others, I have always felt I am being addressed by an infinitely transcendent or numinous Other. Prayer for me is a genuine dialogue or conversation with a Being and not simply some kind of magical incantation or mantra to be repeated frequently for maximum effect.

THE RESPONSE

What is absolutely critical, however, is the next step. Many continue to remain outside the experience of a truly living faith because they never go on to take it. They believe in a personal God as described above but never go on to ask the urgent, existential question: "If such a God exists in and through and behind and over all things, what is my relation to this Reality and what does he want me to do or be?" In spite of my criticism of fundamentalists and conservative evangelicals, I must say they have always seen this particular truth very clearly: You can't simply mouth platitudes about how much you believe in God. If God exists, you need to see the logical necessity of doing something about it. This fact eclipses all others in significance for our lives. The single most important question to be asked is, What response does God require of us?

THE PERENNIAL WISDOM OR PHILOSOPHY

The various religious traditions are largely attempts to answer this question for us. Outwardly, they appear to have very different responses. But my own observations and research have confirmed what many others have also found. Once you pierce beneath the surface trappings, there is an amazing commonality of themes. This is so much the case that religious scholars and philosophers have come to speak of what is called the "Perennial Wisdom" behind most of the major faiths. This can be summed up in various ways but its main outline, with a nod of appreciation to Aldous Huxley (for his preface to a Mentor Book translation of the Bhagavad-Gita) is as follows:

(1) All that is, the entire cosmos, including human consciousness and the billions of far-spun galaxies of outer space, is the expression or incarnation of a Divine Ground of Being, whom we call God. Within it (or rather him) all other realities exist or "hang together" and without it (him) they would have no existence at all. The universe is not God but exists in its entirety in God.

(2) Human beings are capable of knowing about this Divine Ground not just by inference or analogy; a firsthand knowledge is possible through direct intuition, which is superior to normal reasoning. This intuitive step – which is partly what is meant by faith – unites the knower with the Known.

(3) Humans possess a kind of double nature, the ego of day-to-day living and an inner, eternal and higher Self, the spirit which is a spark of divinity or the Divine Ground within. The great Quaker, George Fox, founder of the Society of Friends (1624-91), spoke of this as "that of God in us." By identifying ourselves with this spark of the divine (the "light which gives light to every person coming into the world" of John's Gospel), we can be at one with God or Ultimacy. Some go further and take this

truth to mean that each of us is, in a sense, God. There is a certain logic to this, but it can also sometimes lead to serious confusion. I prefer to speak of God as in us, at the very core of our true Selves.

(4) The true purpose of life on this earth is to discover and identify oneself with this spirit or spark within "and so come to the unitive knowledge of the Divine Ground" or God.

In my book *For Christ's Sake* I have written about how the Church has badly misunderstood the life and teaching of Jesus. Those wanting a fuller account of what I believe about him can find it there. I would simply say here that when you apply the four doctrines of the Perennial Wisdom I have just described to his essential message you will find a lot of things falling into place that may have baffled you before. Jesus called the Divine Ground "Father" and, especially from his baptism on, was deeply conscious of his own unity with him. He believed that entrance into what he called the Kingdom of God was possible for everyone. What's more, he believed it was already within us waiting to be discovered. Jesus stressed that because of this divine spark in every human being, doing a kindness to even the most lowly of all was the same as doing it to him. In other words, God's presence in a person's heart and soul, whether recognized or not by the individual concerned, meant an intrinsic solidarity of every human with every other and therefore with him.

The thing about Jesus that has won near-universal

recognition, even from those who would never call themselves Christians, is that his sense of being at one with the Divine Ground shone through in a unique manner. So much so, in fact, that some of his followers at an early stage after the Easter Event began using language about him they had previously reserved for God alone. Eventually the creeds were formulated and his deity became a matter of essential doctrine. Yet, Jesus himself never claimed to be God in any absolute sense. He simply set forth and lived the Perennial Wisdom in its highest expression. Once, in John's Gospel, when the authorities threaten stoning because he said "I and my Father are one" (their charge reportedly was: "Thou, being a man, makest thyself God"), Jesus quotes their own Hebrew Bible and shows how badly they have misunderstood his point. He asks: "Is it not written in your own law, 'I said, you are gods'?" Since the "you" in this passage refers to the Jewish people themselves, he goes on to show that his sense of being sent by God gives him at least the right to say he is the Son of God. He is surprised they're taking it the wrong way and shouting "blasphemy."

Clearly, Jesus was "filled" with – obedient to – the Spirit in a manner and to an extent that none of us since has managed to approximate. He is friend and master or guru for my own spiritual journey. I believe it would be idolatry, however, to call him God. Jesus lived and died a pious Jew. His message was not about himself but the Kingdom of God. When he was asked what is the greatest commandment, he replied by stating the Shema, which is to this day repeated morning and evening by every devout member of Judaism: "Hear, O Israel; the Lord our God is one Lord: and thou shalt love the Lord thy God with all thine heart, and with all thy soul, and with all thy might."

If you and I recognize our oneness with God and with the whole creation, including not just all other human beings but the animals, the earth and all that is in it or in the heavens around it, it follows that our guiding ethic must be an all-encompassing compassion. To injure anything or anyone is to harm what belongs intimately to ourselves. The natural response to an enlightened sense of who and what we are – and to whom we belong – is to seek to follow what all religions in one way or another refer to as "the Way." It is a way in harmony with the soul of the universe; it seeks justice for all and wholeness. Its hallmark is love. In other words, coming to believe in God is not about finding some safe, inward-looking haven from the storms and shocks of life. It's about living out who we are individually meant to be – as we struggle to help others gain the freedom to do the same.

A Global Ethic

At the core of ethics are compassion and justice. Our best attempts at formulating codes of conduct or morality flow from these twin ideals or principles. The more sensitive we are to each of them, the more likely we are both to know and to do what we ought to, in other words, what is "right."

For secular humanists, agnostics and atheists, the sense of "oughtness" or of morality derives from humans' social needs and is based on enlightened self-interest – on what is useful or best for the greatest number. Compassion and justice, in this view, originate in the need for survival, for the protection of the many from the aggression and hostility of the few. Morality, then, flows from a kind of social contract. It's based upon utilitarian or pragmatic considerations.

For believers in God, the sense of obligation to show love and to act justly is the result of direct revelation. Right and wrong have an objective reality apart from what is or is not useful to the majority. The moral laws come down "from above" in the form of codes such as the Ten Commandments, the Sermon on the Mount, the teachings of the Qur'an and so forth. Conscience, while it can be trained, is essentially (in this view) the quiet voice of God's Spirit prompting us from within to obey the code revealed and imposed from without.

While not denying this religious understanding of morality, I prefer to think of it and express it rather differently. Instead of coming down from on high, so to speak, I believe our sense of obligation to seek what is compassionate and just flows out of the heart of the universe itself. In the story of the giving of the Ten Commandments to Moses or in Jesus' summary of them in the positive form of "love God and love your neighbour as yourself," we have not so much a laying on us of something from outside as a pointing to laws already shining in and throughout the cosmos. In other words, it is really a way of saying this, in fact, is how the universe works. I believe that space, time, matter – and information – the ingredients of the cosmos as we know it, have a moral dimension. There are moral laws as well as physical laws. They can be ignored or disobeyed but only at one's peril. Failure to live by compassion and justice has consequences every bit as certain as the failure to honour the laws of gravity or of electricity.

What matters ultimately, however, is not whose theory of the basis of morality is correct. The real crunch comes over performance. Today, as in the past, compassion and justice are everywhere being mocked or denied on a monumental scale by believers and non-believers alike. The consequences in terms of human – and animal – suffering are staggering. So much unnecessary cruelty, pain and death; so much terror, hardship, torture, oppression, hunger and disease; so much fighting and hate. Despite the aggressiveness of some religions and the wishful thinking of certain idealists, there will never be one world faith to which all subscribe. Nor would it be desirable in any case. God must love diversity or it wouldn't be the salient feature of the whole panoply of nature. No two snowflakes are exactly alike, no two animals, no two faces, two trees, or two stars.

Yet, some deep bond is needed if humanity is to move ahead into the next millennium without destroying itself or the planet. If there is to be community either locally or globally, there have to be building blocks out of which community flows. The word community itself comes from holding things in common. Without things held in common, there can be no community, only competition, enmity, and strife. The most urgent question for a multicultural, heterogeneous society like Canada, and for the world of which it is a microcosm, is how to find some key, common values on which a harmonious community can be built while still preserving our differences.

It is possible, and thankfully we don't all have to become Christians, Muslims, Baha'is or Buddhists to achieve it. We can be religious or non-religious and still adopt a universal, global ethic based upon the highest instincts of our race. There already is a single ethical principle which appears not just in all the world's great religions but also in its best secular philosophies. We call it the Golden Rule. You need no specific, supernatural authority to see its rightness or to live by it. In its most popular form it says simply: "Do as you would be done by." It occurs in the poetry of the Greek writer, Hesiod (circa 700 B.C.): "He harms himself who does harm to another, and the evil plan is most harmful to the planner." Aristotle (384-322 B.C.) had a more limited version and put it this way: "We should behave to our friends as we would wish our friends to behave to us."

Confucius (551-479 B.C.) is credited as the first to phrase it in the classic form, albeit negatively: "What you do not want done to yourself, do not unto others."

It occurs in all the world's major religions:

• Christianity: "Therefore all things whatsoever ye would that men should do to you, do ye even so to them; For this is the law and the prophets."

• Judaism: "What is hateful to you, do not to your fellowmen." (The Talmud says it's the whole Law. "All the rest is commentary.")

• Islam: "No one of you is a believer until he desires for his brother that which he desires for himself."

• Hinduism: "Do nothing to others which would cause you pain if done to you."

• Buddhism: "Hurt not others in ways that you yourself would find hurtful."

• Taoism: "Regard your neighbour's gain as your own gain and your neighbour's loss as your own loss."

According to Confucius, the entire principle can be summed up in the single word "*shu*," reciprocity.

Coupled with the Golden Rule is what I believe is the second essential value for any universal, global ethic – non-violence. Here there is less overall consensus. But, if humanity is ever to move away from ethnic hatreds and from the horrors of war – indeed if it is to survive – all of us must come to see what some of the greatest moral leaders of the past have always seen – that violence, however seemingly justified, only provokes more violence and solves nothing. One can argue that there have been just wars in the past, but the nature of modern warfare has rendered that dubious notion irrelevant today. Jesus saw the need for non-violence; Gandhi saw it (he said: "Non-violence is the first article of my faith"); Martin Luther King saw it; and we must come to see it too.

These two values, the Golden Rule and the principle of non-violence, provide a firm basis both for the possibility of global peace and for harmony in the classroom, work place, family and neighbourhood. I believe they should be taught in our schools, extolled in the media, and unceasingly trumpeted by all churches, synagogues and temples, and that every humanist and atheist organization should lend its weight as well. We have been sitting for too long upon a vast and largely unexploited resource for the common good!

THE ONE-WAY DOGMA

Unfortunately, most – though not all – religions have succumbed to the seduction of believing and teaching they are the sole or the vastly superior way to God. Some are like the elderly Anglican who said: "Well, there may be other ways to God, but no gentleman would take them." I believe it is possible to be connected to God or "enlightened" without active participation in any formal or organized religion at all. God is not a Jew, a Christian, a Muslim or a Mormon. And yet, as have many others, I have found it helpful to have a home community and a specific tradition to which I belong. I consider myself to be a struggling Christian who has found the Anglican Church the most conducive to his own spiritual growth. But, I'm attached to it by an elastic band, not a chain.

If you are a believer, you can use almost any spiritual tradition and find growth within it. Personally, I have learned much from a host of non-Anglican and non-Christian saints, sages and sacred texts. I can feel at home at the worship of any major faith. There is no right denomination, faith or sect for everyone. As noted already, the God who made not one kind of tree but thousands of different varieties and who has made not one shade of green but a myriad of subtly differing shades has declared a love of multiplicity and of individuation that is cosmic in scale. So it makes no sense at all that there should be only one way to come to him, to worship him, or to live in his service. Imagine yourself on Mars, looking back on the blue ball of Earth. From that perspective, the idea that some groups and individuals on this fragile planet think that they alone know and hold the truth about ultimate reality is patently ludicrous. I have long been convinced that the idea that there is no salvation outside this or that religion or church was born more out of fear and a lust for control over people's hearts, minds and bodies than from any true understanding of the mind and will of the Creator.

PRAYER

Prayer, like gravity, is an unseen force. Yet, it's prodigiously powerful and reaches to the ends of the earth. Sceptics can scoff and atheists argue that it's merely talking to oneself. But I believe they are dead wrong. There's a reason why prayer is a universal phenomenon both ancient and modern. There's a reason why it's as instinctual as the urge to survive itself. A human being is by nature a praying being. We pray because we need to and because it works! I know it to be so. This knowing is based on personal experience as well as upon years of observing it working in the lives of many others.

This is not a claim to any total understanding of prayer. In that respect I feel like a child playing on the shore of some vast, unknown continent. So do those whom I respect and who are far more advanced in prayer than I. But, I have come to believe more strongly than ever before that Alfred, Lord Tennyson was right when he penned the line: "More things are wrought by prayer than this world dreams of."

Prayer is not magic – where you say this or that formula to God and out pops the answer you want. We have all prayed, sometimes agonizingly, for certain things, results, or conditions – for ourselves or for others – and the answer has either been a resounding no or, worse still, silence. Though we would very much like it to be so, prayer is not just one more automated control switch or piece of software in our plethora of technological gimmickry. It operates according to its own invisible laws, according to the Will of God. It is always answered, but the answer comes according to a higher law of love than we can easily hear or see. This is why one of the simplest and best prayers is "Thy will be done" in any particular situation. Jesus himself used it not just in the Lord's Prayer but also during his agony in Gethsemane. True, often this is offered in a spirit of resignation or fatalism, but I'm not talking about that. I'm talking about a positive affirmation, an acknowledgement that the whole of life is ultimately in God's hands and that he knows what is best for us. In the end, as T. S. Eliot puts it: "All shall be well and all manner of things shall be well."

What interests me is that while polls show the majority of ordinary people believe in the reality and power of prayer, the secular scientific and medical establishments carry on for the most part ignoring it completely. For example, pharmaceutical companies in North America are spending as much as $15 billion (US) a year to try to come up with a new antibiotic to combat the "superbacteria" that have evolved in response to previous antibiotics. Of course, any fresh antibiotic will have more side effects and will eventually be rendered obsolete by fresh bacterial mutations. They will spend absolutely nothing, naturally, on research into the effects of prayer upon health and healing. You can't put that into a pill and mass-market it. Yet, recent research I did for my book on healing, *The Uncommon Touch*, showed me that prayer has a measurable effect on healing. The medical establishment could put protocols in place to make a beginning at least of documenting the effects of prayer scientifically.

In 1975, Dr. Herbert Benson, a cardiologist and professor of medicine at Harvard University, wrote the book *The Relaxation Response*. He followed it with *The Mind/Body Effect*, and in 1984 with *Beyond the Relaxation Response*. In his research into the physical effects of meditation and prayer, Benson has found and documented that the "Faith Factor," as he calls it, makes a profound difference to human health. Writing not as a proponent of any particular religious point of view but as a scientist, Benson says that the regular use of specific faith affirmations (such as, "God is my refuge and strength," or "I am one with God") or simple prayer words in meditation can have a "quantifiable, scientifically measurable effect" on the body. For example, in *Beyond the Relaxation Response* he tells how he and a team of scientists recorded the ability of certain Buddhist monks in India to raise their skin temperature by as much as fifteen degrees Fahrenheit through meditation and prayer.

You may already have read of the experiments done by cardiologist Dr. Randolph Byrd, formerly a professor at the University of California. I described them in *The Uncommon Touch*. Using tight controls, Byrd randomly designated about four hundred coronary care patients at San Francisco General Hospital into one of two groups. One group (192 patients) were prayed for regularly by home prayer groups and the others (201) were not. In every other way they were treated normally by the hospital staff. Dr. Larry Dossey, in *Recovering the Soul: A Scientific and Spiritual Search*, described Byrd's methods as the most rigid that can be used in clinical studies in medicine – "a randomized, double-blind experiment in which neither the patients, nurses, nor doctors knew which group the patients were in." Byrd recruited Protestants and Catholics across the United States to pray for the first group. They were given their names and a little information about their condition and were asked to pray daily. Each patient in the first group was on the list of between five and seven volunteers.

The results of the ten-month study were remarkable. Those prayed for differed from the others in several striking ways: they were five times less likely to need antibiotics; they were three times less likely to develop pulmonary edema (fluid on the lungs due to heart failure); none of them needed intubation (twelve in the non-prayed-for group had to have ventilatory support); and fewer of them died during the study. Dossey comments: "If the technique had been a new drug or procedure . . . it would . . . have been heralded as some kind of break-through." One otherwise sceptical doctor, impressed by Byrd's methods and the results, has commented: "Maybe we doctors should be writing on our order sheets, 'Pray three times a day.' If it works, it works." Byrd's study does not stand alone. Yet, much more research could and should be done. There are no side effects and the cost, as in the case of the energy called love, is nil.

Recently, I came across another surprising set of experiments, done under the most rigorous of scientific protocols, by a priest from San Francisco, Rev. Dr. Sean O'Laoire. The research project, "An Experimental Study of the Effects of Intercessory Prayer-at-a-distance on Self-esteem, Anxiety and Depression," was done at the Institute of Transpersonal Psychology, Palo Alto, California. It was written up as a successful, but as yet unpublished, doctoral thesis.

This too was a controlled, randomized, double-blind study of the effect of prayer on mood, self-esteem, anxiety, depression, and other indicators of psychological ill health. O'Laoire used 496 adult volunteers; of these, 90 offered to be the "agents" or the ones doing the praying, and the "subjects" were divided – without being told who was who – into a control group of 147 and a group of 259 who would be prayed for. Incidentally, all the subjects were promised that if the experiment showed positive results, then those not prayed for, the control group, would subsequently be prayed for.

The agents were given photographs and the names of their subjects, and committed themselves to praying for them for fifteen minutes daily for twelve weeks. All 496 participants were given five approved, standard psychological tests before the twelve-week period began. The final results showed "significant improvement" in the subjects in all the categories tested: the amount of self-esteem, the levels of both state and trait anxiety; the amount of depression; and the extent of mood disorders in general. In addition, subjective testing showed there was improvement also in how those prayed for felt about their relationships, creativity, spirituality, and overall physical, emotional and intellectual well-being.

There is more to O'Laoire's findings than I can relate in this brief account. But, as with Byrd's, his results are such that had they been secured with a new drug or medical technique, they would have been hailed as a major discovery. However, it is largely the pharmaceutical industry that pays for the advertising in medical journals – and for the bulk of medical research in general. I believe it is for this reason that O'Laoire's findings have so far been greeted with silence.

I'm convinced that nothing is more crucial, not just to our health, but also to the maturing of our spirituality, than prayer. But, it's important to understand that prayer is not so much what we say, how we say it or where, in our "conversation" with God. What is vital is the focusing of one's attention – a kind of tuning of the whole inner self towards the Creator of our being and of the cosmos. We know, for example, that however silent and alone we may be in our room, our car, or the outdoors, there are transmissions of thousands of signals flooding the space around us all the time. We have only to turn on a radio, television or other receiver to be in touch with these invisible voices and images. The finer the tuning, the clearer the communication. True prayer is much like that. It's a reaching out to a Presence already there. The very act of so doing is transformative whether we pray for others or ourselves. At its highest level, prayer consists less of asking and much more of simple listening in stillness.

I like kneeling in church at times, praying where, as T. S. Eliot wrote, "Prayer has been valid." But, I especially like to pray when I'm walking alone. There is something about being outdoors and surrounded by nature that permits my spirit to relax and to soar a little. When I want to verbalize rather than to listen, I've found it helpful to pray aloud, but softly lest others think the worst! Many find a certain position – for example, sitting crosslegged on the floor – necessary for disciplined meditation or prayer. No one way works for everyone. We have to work at it until we discover what's best for ourselves and ignore any rigid rules laid down by experts or various spiritual traditions.

The New Testament has a rather enigmatic command to "pray without ceasing." Some have taken this quite literally and have taught prayers or mantras to be repeated mentally every second of the waking day. But most biblical scholars take the text to mean: "Have an attitude of prayer in all you do or say." This means that everything – one's work, play, relationships and goals – is ultimately seen as part of God's concern. The whole of life is then seen in the light of the Eternal. Nothing brings greater meaning or depth to life than that. That's the secret of prayer.

THE FUNDAMENTAL ENEMY

"To conquer fear is the beginning of wisdom." (Bertrand Russell)

"Perfect love casts out fear." (The New Testament)

Many people think that the Bible says the greatest obstacle to human happiness is sin in one form or another. In fact, Christianity has through the centuries been obsessed with sin and with our need for some outside redemption from it. A great deal of cruelty, guilt and misery have flowed as a result. For many years, I knew there was something distorted about this emphasis on sin and about the doctrine of the total depravity of human beings – including newborn babies – but, I didn't get it into focus properly until one day I read a booklet by the Scottish philosopher John Macmurray – *To Save from Fear* (1964). Macmurray, who became a Quaker because of the traditional churches' acceptance of war, said that when he first read the Gospels in an objective way, laying aside the dogma and teaching that had accumulated around them, he was amazed. He discovered that, contrary to what he had been taught, Jesus' main preoccupation was not with sin at all. His attitude to sin was that it was to be repented of, forgiven, and let go – without need of clergy, rites or whatever. The real enemy of humankind, according to Jesus, Macmurray found, was fear and its comrades, anxiety, worry, and lack of trust.

Macmurray's words hit me like a lightning bolt and I couldn't wait to read the four Gospels afresh for myself. Putting aside all I had learned in Sunday School, from thousands of sermons, from theological college and from books, I picked up my Greek New Testament (I was teaching Greek at the time) and began reading with new eyes. I quickly found that Jesus' most characteristic saying, his signature slogan, was "Be not afraid," "Be of good courage" or "Have confidence." He talked continually about the need for faith – faith, however, not in the sense of mental assent to certain creeds, propositions, or other religiously correct opinions – but in the radical sense of a deep trust in life, the universe and the reality he called "Father." The thing that puzzled him most about both his disciples and the people of his time was why they had so little faith or trust.

This experience had an enormous impact on my thinking about the Christian message itself. Two questions, nevertheless, remained: Is fear indeed the central problem for humanity, and, if so, how is it to be dealt with? How can it be replaced by faith, confidence and trust? Certainly nothing can rival fear when it comes to the corrosion of our inner poise, peace and happiness. There are obvious fears like the fear of a specific illness, fear of death, our own or of our loved ones, fear of losing one's job, fear of failing at some task, fear of loneliness, fear of being afraid. But, there are a thousand other subtle fears that plague us and rob us of tranquillity. And they can make us do things both strange and terrible.

Racism is based upon fear, fear of the unknown, fear of being diminished in some way or of losing out to strangers. The obscenity of militarism, unceasing production and sales of ever more deadly weaponry, and war itself are accompanied by greed, lust for power and a host of other evils, but at base they arise from fear – fear of one's neighbour, fear of not being number one, fear of loss of influence or of being taken over. At the root of most of the injustice responsible for the numbing suffering we witness daily in the news is fear. The fanatical fundamentalism evident today in so many regions of the world is the product of fear – fear of change, fear of uncertainty, fear of losing one's identity, fear of thinking for oneself. We are living through a time when people's hearts "are failing them for fear."

But, telling people who are bound by one or more fears they should simply relax and "be of good courage" or trust the universe is no help. It's a bit like advising someone caught in an acute depression to cheer up. Clearly, Jesus did not engage in such folly. His confrontation with fear in his own life and that of others was made possible through his overwhelming conviction that God could be trusted at all times, even through death. This was not some abstract, intellectual belief on his part. It was based upon his core spiritual experience, told, for example, in the symbolism of his baptism in Jordan, where he is said to have seen the heavens open and to have heard a voice saying, "This is my beloved son."

Assured by this experience that he was truly the child of God, he was filled by an awareness of being totally loved by "the Father" of all. It was his experience of a Presence at the heart of life and of being wholly grasped by that Presence that gave him the assurance to conquer fear. "Perfect love casts out fear." That doesn't mean our perfect love for God. Nobody has that. It's trusting God's perfect love for us that changes things. To the extent that we accept that, we can trust life, ourselves and each other. We can begin, perhaps haltingly at first, to let go and to say farewell to fear.

THE NEED TO DOUBT

"I have too many doubts about God, faith or spiritual things; I'd feel like a total hypocrite in a church, synagogue, temple or mosque." I hear this kind of thing constantly from good people, many with a deep, wistful longing to believe, who feel disqualified from having a living faith because of their doubts. At the same time, countless numbers of others who think of themselves as believers, see doubt as a kind of mortal enemy to be feared and shunned. Doubt, they feel, will crush the walls of the fortress of faith like a battering ram or silently corrode the foundations like some hidden rot or biting rust.

Both of these groups are the victims of a tragic misunderstanding. It's one for which the various religions must shoulder the blame. They have either taught directly or have implied that to doubt is to sin or to stray from the truth. It's like tempting God. I believe that, on the contrary, doubt is faith's strongest ally and friend. More than that even, it's an essential component of each individual's own "faith journey." Show me someone in any faith who says he or she never doubts and I'll show you someone who hasn't grown an inch spiritually since they first believed. Indeed, one of the greatest problems religious institutions face today is that far too many believers are walking around with an anemic parody of mature belief – a kind of Sunday School variety – and it fails utterly at a time of crisis.

Very few can follow media accounts of the tragedies, the crimes, the injustices and the follies of our world on the one hand and learn something of the explosion of scientific information about every aspect of life and the cosmos on the other and not have doubts. Who can sit by the bedside of a loved one ravaged by some cruel, killing disease and not know doubt? You can't preside, as I have often done, at the funeral of a child and not feel a pang of uncertainty as to the love or justice of God. But it is in the very act of facing such doubts, agonizing over them and seeking a better understanding that we gain a deeper faith to carry on.

I remember, as a student, going through a long period when I could no longer say the words in the Creed: "And, I believe in the resurrection of the body." I had said them by rote for years. Then one day I thought about what I was saying and I realized I had real doubts about its truth. I started to keep silent at that part of the service and began a serious attempt to get at the meaning behind the surface, literal sense which had become so meaningless to me. Naively, I had thought that as some people are cremated, some are blown apart in war or virtually evaporated by a nuclear blast, their bodies could not be resurrected. It took some time before I realized that the Christian message is not about resurrection of corpses but about the "raising up" of the spiritual body into a new plane of being. We will not be gibbering ghosts or hollow shades in the life to come but embodied beings –

"God giveth it a body." My doubts as a student sowed the seeds for an investigation many years later into the whole subject of life after death which eventually resulted in a book.

It was C. S. Lewis's doubts about the whole concept of faith and of Christianity in particular which led him to become one of the best-known apologists for such belief in this century. Some of you – many of you, I hope – have seen the film *Shadowlands*, starring Anthony Hopkins as Lewis and Debra Winger as the divorced woman he married very late in life (Joy Davidman) and then lost so tragically to cancer. The film concentrates on the poignancy and tenderness of their short-lived marriage. It's a truly sensitive and, in the best sense, romantic look at two people of deep faith caught in a web of joy, of suffering and of numbing grief. What is most helpful and moving about this particular drama is the way in which Lewis's grief over his wife's death is played out. You really feel his desolation and his doubt over where, if at all, God can possibly be in all of it. Lewis, as we know from his book *A Grief Observed*, finally moved through and beyond this doubt to a yet maturer faith; but it was a costly, often bitter struggle.

Doubt squarely faced is always a stepping stone to firmer ground, emotionally and intellectually. That's why I call that kind of uncertainty "creative doubt." It forces us to go beyond our old boundaries. Spirituality, or faith, is never a static thing, a defending of old borders. Instead, it's an ongoing dialectic or inner discussion between doubting and believing that moves us ahead. True faith always has an element of agnosticism, of "I don't know – yet." Long ago, Paul put it this way: "For now we see through a glass, darkly; but then face to face: now I know in part; but then shall I know even as I am known."

3

Blocks to Belief

When it comes to matters of faith, spirituality and religion, there are almost as many questions or doubts as there are people, and sometimes these doubts become impediments to belief. To find out what difficulties are commonly encountered today, I decided to ask the readers of my syndicated newspaper column on ethics and religion for their assistance. Accordingly, at the end of my column of November 6, 1994, I made the following appeal:

> It would assist me greatly in my research if readers who would like to have a vital faith in God (regardless of denomination or religion) but honestly cannot because of some question, doubt or other difficulty, would write briefly stating what the block seems to be.

Scores of letters started to come in – and continued to for many weeks – from across the country.

While no two were the same, it eventually became possible to file most of them under a dozen or so headings. In what follows, I propose to try to deal with what seemed to be the most important of them. While remaining faithful to the overall thrust and content of each letter quoted here, I have edited them to make the writer's point as succinct as possible.

Is Belief in God Unscientific?

"Although I was raised in a traditionally religious home, I stopped believing in God while I was still in high school and not long after I had been confirmed. Now in my mid-forties, I feel the lack of some kind of spiritual direction or meaning in my life. Yet, so much of what I was taught as a child seems to be directly contradicted by modern science that I find the idea of believing in some kind of personal God just about impossible. Since it can't be verified by experiment, can't be seen or proved in any way, the 'God hypothesis' seems an anachronism."

This man's sentiments were echoed by many of my respondents and he articulates one of the key problems for faith today. We are so thoroughly surrounded now by technologies and paradigms that are the result of scientific thinking that we have been almost blinded to any other dimension of being. However, the spiritual hunger currently surfacing on all sides bears eloquent testimony to how damaging and limiting this blinkered outlook has been to our deeper psyche. Here, then, is my attempt to address this writer's concern.

Consider. Sometimes we cry when our hearts are breaking with grief. Sometimes we cry for sheer joy. In either case, we produce tears. If we want to know what a tear is or why we have the ability to cry, we can go to science for an answer. The scientist will weigh it, measure it, put it under a microscope, analyze its various molecular components, and test the factors that induced it. His or her final reply, greatly simplified, will run something like this: A tear is a small quantity of saline solution, secreted by the lachrymal glands, under certain specific physical or emotional stimuli.

But, when the scientist has finished all this probing, we'll still have very little idea of what a tear really is or represents. To know the full meaning of tears you have to go to the great poets, the best novelists, and above all to the theologians and to sacred texts. I think of that familiar passage in the Book of Revelation: "God shall wipe away all tears from their eyes; and there shall be no more death, neither sorrow, nor crying," or the wisdom in this excerpt from Nikolai Gogol's novel *Dead Souls*: "And for a long time yet, led by some wondrous power, I am fated to journey hand in hand with my strange heroes and to survey the immensity of life, to survey it through the laughter that all can see and through tears unseen and unknown by anyone." Or again, one hears those thundering words of Winston Churchill in his very first statement to the British House of Commons on becoming prime minister, May 13, 1940: "I have nothing to offer but blood, toil, tears and sweat."

In short, science is one way – and a very important one – of looking at the world, *but it is not the only way*. It can tell us a very great deal about the natural order, but it cannot tell us all we need and want to know. If you believe it can, then you are subscribing to what is technically called "scientism" – the cult of science – and not to proper science itself. This is an extremely important point because in the eyes of many today, especially young people, science is a kind of god. Unless something can be "proved" scientifically, then it's thought to be part of an unreal or imaginary world. This is emphatically not the view of true science. Its claims are much more modest. It can often (though not always) tell us how this or that came to be and how it operates but it cannot tell us the final answer. When it comes to questions of ultimate meaning and purpose, it must give way to other voices.

For centuries, almost since the dawn of the modern era, many have looked at science and religion or spirituality as though they were mutually exclusive. That has never been true, and the fallacy of their supposed incompatibility stands clearly exposed today. In recent decades, in fact, science and spiritual truths have been coming ever closer. Nowadays, if you read any physics, you'll know that when it comes now to describing the subatomic world, the very stuff of the universe, scientists are beginning to use terms once thought peculiar to mysticism alone. For example, the idea that God created the universe out of nothing, as mystics believe, was once ridiculed by many scientists. In the new science of quantum physics, we are told this is going on all the time. The same is true of astrophysicists today when they try to describe the origins of the cosmos. I'm not saying science proves spiritual or religious truth. It's not about that. But it certainly doesn't contradict it. There is absolutely no contradiction, for example, between the biblical doctrine of creation and some variant of Charles Darwin's theory of evolution. In spite of the stance of certain television evangelists on this issue, and in spite of the attempts by so-called Creationists to overthrow or subvert school curriculums in the name of God by introducing their theories of a "young universe," there is no real conflict. The Bible asserts that God made the whole of the universe, including humans, but it is not, nor does it claim to be, a scientific treatise on how it all came to pass.

Its broad strokes are accurate: there are parallels between the current theory of the "Big Bang" and God's "utterance" of the fiat "Let there be light," and it's true that all life (as both science and Genesis agree) came originally from the primal waters which at first covered the earth. But the actual, detailed *how* is best described by science alone. If, as I believe, it took many millions of years for humans to evolve from the rest of the animals, this to me is not less marvellous, less God-driven, than some instantaneous, literal, coming to be from the dust; indeed, it's infinitely more amazing still.

I will close this discussion with a brief parable. I'm fully aware of its limitations (theologians should never be this smug!) but it contains a valuable truth. A group of scientists had laboured for many years to climb up a tall mountain called Knowledge. When they got to the top they met some theologians already there having tea. The theologians quipped: "Greetings. What took you so long?"

Those who can't believe because of science need to think again.

THE PROBLEM OF MIRACLES

"I am a twenty-year-old university student majoring in philosophy. The idea of a God who is the Intelligence behind all things – like Aristotle's Unmoved Mover or who is the sum of all the laws governing the universe – seems to me unavoidable. What I cannot accept is the concept of a God who actively intervenes in human affairs. This difficulty becomes really focused when religious people talk about miracles."

This young woman raises a question that was brought up or touched upon by a number of the respondents. The subject is enormous – C. S. Lewis wrote an interesting but, in the end, rather unsatisfactory book about it with the simple title *Miracles* some forty years ago. Here is a much briefer account of some of my own reflections:

At the time of writing this, I had just read a newspaper story of how Pat Burns, the coach of the Toronto Maple Leafs hockey team, had a message for his young goaltender, Felix "the Cat" Potvin, shortly before a recent match against the Dallas Stars. Having learned that his top defenceman, Dave Ellett, would be off with an injury for six weeks, Burns told Potvin he'd better "get his bag of miracles out." After the game, in which Potvin shone and the Leafs squeaked out a 3–2 win, Burns told reporters: "He had two miracle periods and then starts the third by letting one in. We'll forgive him for that." This use of the word miracle is commonplace. We all know what is meant. Burns wasn't hoping or asking for a supernatural event. He meant simply that his goalie would have to be at or beyond his best to make up for the hole in the Leaf defence left by Ellett's absence. To say Potvin had "two miracle periods" is simply another way of saying his performance was outstanding, a source of wonderment.

The Latin noun, *miraculum*, comes from a verb root meaning "to marvel or wonder at." So, a miracle is literally anything that evokes awe. In its religious sense, however, a miracle denotes an act of divine intervention. According to *The Oxford Dictionary of the Christian Church*, a miracle is "a sensible fact produced by the special intervention of

God for a religious end, transcending the normal order of things usually termed the Law of Nature." While Protestant orthodoxy usually confines itself to belief in the miracles of the Bible, Catholic orthodoxy holds that miracles have at all times occurred within the pale of the Church. In canon law, between two and four authenticated miracles after death are required for the beatification of a saint, although belief in any of these non-biblical miracles is not an essential of the faith.

It's important we think clearly about this matter because few other concepts have caused more perplexity and confusion for believers and non-believers alike over the years. If God actively, and seemingly arbitrarily, intervenes from time to time to suspend, contradict or bypass the natural laws of the universe, the already difficult notion of divine justice and mercy – in the face of unmerited suffering and pain – becomes virtually incomprehensible. In other words, if God can break his own imposed order, the question of why he doesn't in any particularly agonizing situation becomes unbearably acute.

My own admittedly limited understanding approaches this matter from what may seem to be an unorthodox position, but to date it is the only one that makes sense to me. In the abstract, of course, God can do anything God wants to. So, miracles in the traditional view cannot simply be ruled out absolutely. It is a fallacy to decide beforehand that miracles are an impossibility and then, after much argument, conclude they don't happen! As Supreme First Cause of all things, God could conceivably be responsible for the laws of nature but not himself subject to them. Arbitrary or routine intervention would then be an open option. But, apart from raising the issue of why, on this view, God appears to play favourites among species and among humans, intervening for this person or that group but not for others – the case of the lone survivor of the downed jet who exults "God gave me a miracle!" comes to mind – it seems to contradict our increasing scientific knowledge. While it is true that the more we think we know the larger are the mysteries of the cosmos, nevertheless each new discovery strips away old "miracles." What was once a miracle in the strict religious sense is now "perfectly natural."

The return of spring is a miracle. The birth of a baby is a miracle. Our immune system is a miracle. The thunderstorm or the earthquake are miracles. But, we now know the causes and principles at work in each of these. They don't require belief in divine intervention to be understood. I am convinced that one day we will recognize that while we are surrounded by miracles there are no miracles in the traditional sense. To put it as clearly as possible, in my view, a supposed religious miracle is really an event whose underlying laws we have yet to comprehend. As the well-known Christian healer Agnes Sandford once put it: "God always works lawfully." Yesterday's miracle is today's fresh leap of knowledge.

The reason, for example, that prayer is such a powerful force in human affairs is not that it sometimes persuades a reluctant Deity to perform supernatural miracles on behalf of some and not of others. Rather, it is itself – or it releases and focuses – a kind of subtle energy or form of communication yet to be fully understood. This also holds true, I'm convinced, of the hidden powers of healing vested in traditional healers and attested to, for example, in the New Testament. Recent research shows clearly that there are subtle energies involved in such healing that can be shown by their effects, under laboratory conditions, even though as yet there is no way of discerning their precise nature. (I refer the reader to my book *The Uncommon Touch* for an account of the scientific evidence of this.) The laws governing these energies remain a mystery. But, since science still doesn't know precisely how Aspirin works or how to cure the common cold, our present ignorance doesn't worry me at all.

However, none of the above means that I am a Deist – one who sees the universe as having been made by God and then left to run on its own, the way a watch-maker makes a clock. God doesn't have to make special interventions because he is already and always within, through, and under the whole process of creation – closer to us than our own thoughts and feelings. It is when we, knowingly or unknowingly, act or think or pray according to the laws of the Spirit that "miracles" occur.

GOD AND GUILT

"I would like to believe but was raised Catholic in the sixties in Spain. Even then I didn't feel comfortable with the Pope claiming to be infallible and the head of the only true church. In particular, it seemed that everything related to sex was somehow dirty with the result that, growing up, we always felt guilty and afraid. A religion that makes you feel guilty if you don't believe blindly or because you want a glimmer of rationality simply ends up by alienating people like me."

There are a number of questions here but I want to deal with guilt in general and guilt over sexuality in particular. Unquestionably, there are millions of people today who have been left with unwarranted guilt feelings because of their religious upbringing. I meet them or hear from them every day. In my long experience, I have found that no religious tradition is wholly free from having foisted a burden of guilt on its followers. But Judaism and Christianity seem to have been the worst offenders. It would seem that the Judeo-Christian God specializes in guilt. Indeed, evangelists both on television and elsewhere still use the technique of first inducing feelings of guilt in their flock and then pulling out their version of "the Gospel" as the remedy. The Christian martyr, Dietrich Bonhoeffer (executed by the Nazis in 1945), warned against this kind of spiritual quackery in his *Letters from Prison*, but it's still much in vogue today.

There is, of course, a place for guilt. The human

being who has no sense of remorse or guilt for wrong-doing is a potentially quite dangerous psychopath. However, one of the products of years of pop psychology and innumerable self-help books has been the widespread fallacy that any kind of guilt is harmful to our development and is to be avoided or purged immediately. The result of this notion can be seen in the increasing number of horrific crimes committed by people, even children, who are apparently totally devoid of remorse or feelings of any kind. The ability to feel guilt – especially when we have hurt others in some way – is part of what it means to be a moral person. It's essential to our own humanity.

What we are discussing here, however, are unmerited or unfounded feelings of unworthiness and remorse. The doctrine that we are by our very birth and nature part of a corrupt and depraved continuum called humanity, that we are sinners simply by virtue of sharing in "original sin" has done terrible harm to children and adults alike. It is truly staggering to realize that in North America today, in spite of the fact that the airwaves are filled with religious messages day and night, and that people attend religious services as on few other continents, the number-one personal problem North Americans have is an inability to feel good about themselves, of feeling accepted at the depth of their being.

When it comes to sex, in their anxiety to protect and exalt this special gift of the Creator – and, let's be honest, also in a desire to assert and maintain control – religious leaders have gone far too far. Their message to the world has been fearsome and extremely negative. In my book *The Divine Lover: A Celebration of Romantic Love*, I have tried to set out the case for seeing sexual intimacy itself as a way of knowing and meeting God. I point out the irony that the one truly erotic piece of writing in the Bible, the Song of Songs, has been so spiritualized by both Jews and Christians it has been emptied of its positive view of sexuality and romantic love almost entirely. The near-obsession of the Roman Catholic Church and other churches with prohibitions and reservations over sexual conduct is not only wrong-headed, it is counter-productive. Nothing has done more to alienate the present generation of young people from religion than the churches' failure to articulate a positive and sensible doctrine of the body and of sexuality.

The problems of false guilt and of thinking of sex as "dirty" are not "God problems" at all. They arise from warped, man-made teaching promulgated in the name of God but that has little to do with either reason or true faith. This is not to say that you can adopt the "anything goes" approach to sex and pretend to be following the will of God. There are moral criteria which apply here as they do elsewhere; for example, the law of compassion, of not doing harm, or of not using others as objects rather than meeting them in mutuality as subjects. There are matters of commitment and of full equality. But, if there is a God, sex is his creation, and to suggest it is otherwise than "very good" is the real sexual sin.

JESUS THE ONLY WAY?

"My wife and I were both raised in the Lutheran Church, Missouri Synod. While we could only be described now as nominal Christians, having left off church-going many years ago, we are increasingly aware of being spiritually hungry. We would like to have a meaningful faith in God but are put off by many things – most notably by the claim of Christianity to be the only way to salvation. I know from your columns that you take a different approach but how do you get around the verse drummed into us when we were active church members: 'I am the Way the Truth and the Life. No man cometh unto the Father but by me'?"

As I suggested earlier, the greatest curse of religion as a force in the world is and has been that too many adherents of this or that faith fervently believe theirs is the sole possessor of the fullness of THE TRUTH. Few things cause more global dissension and rancour than this. Nothing is more contrary to the urgent need today for tolerance and societal harmony. It is the enemy of peace.

Most if not all faiths have conservative elements that cling to the "one truth" ideology. But the funda-mentalist wings of Judaism, Christianity and Islam outstrip all others in their zeal. Since I know it best and since it is still – nominally at any rate – the faith held by the majority in the West, I will deal here with Christianity's claims to absolute superiority. The ultra-orthodox and the conservatives in all branches, from Billy Graham to the Pope, while perhaps admitting there are "rays of light" or "seeds of the truth" in other faiths, adamantly maintain that theirs is the final and fullest revelation of God.

The key text cited by all who believe this is quoted by the writer of this letter. It comes from John's Gospel, where Jesus apparently says that there is no other access to God than through him. It seems wholly categorical. If this unique passage is taken literally, it provides a charter for conservative Christians to look down from great heights on everybody else. Historically, in fact, it has often been used as justification to coerce and even use violence against those who didn't happen to agree or to accept it. The Spanish Inquisition is just one example.

What are we to make of such a claim? A proper answer requires work. The first question to examine is, did Jesus actually make such a pronouncement? If he did, and if, as the conservatives also insist, he was indeed none other than the Second Person of the Holy Trinity, God-in-the-flesh, then obviously all people who call themselves Christian are bound to take it as gospel truth. The rest follows logically. But, even apart from the fact that the doctrine of the Trinity is not to be found in the Bible but emerged in the early centuries of the church (see *For Christ's Sake*), there are solid grounds for thinking that the historical Jesus never uttered this exclusionary saying at all.

To understand this, we have to take a small detour into New Testament scholarship. The Gospel of John is the only one of the four where Jesus makes this claim. The next question to be asked, then, is what is the nature and status of this Gospel? Almost from the time it was written – probably between 80 and 95 A.D., although nobody really knows for certain – John's Gospel has been regarded as quite different from the other three, which are known as the Synoptic Gospels because their outlook and stories have so much in common. John was received into the canon or official list of books of the New Testament only after considerable debate. In the second century, Clement of Alexandria (150-215 A.D.) called it a "spiritual" gospel because it reads much more like an inspired meditation on the meaning of the Christ Event than an attempt at factual recording.

Because of space, I can only invite you to read this Gospel and then peruse any one of the other three. I think you will quickly see that there are two different worlds here. Not only is the chronology different; the entire style and the way Jesus is presented are almost entirely at variance. Either Jesus spoke in short pithy aphorisms and in parables, as the Synoptics portray him, or he spoke in the highly contrived, Greek-style monologues given by John. Either he was modest and elusive regarding his claims to being the Messiah and to being the sole Son of God, as the first three

Gospels report, or he was a man who made bold and near-blasphemous statements about himself from the very outset of his ministry and literally "walked three feet above the ground," as one critical scholar has said. While there is some solid topographical and chronological detail in John, the book does indeed read much more like a meditation aimed at producing deeper faith than as a record of what Jesus actually said and did. In other words, it is, as indeed it says of itself (20:31), a work composed specifically with persuasion in mind. Not only that, but also it was written at a time of bitter polemics between the early Christians and official Judaism. When you realize the author was himself a Jew (a Hellenized Jew), you know that his frequent negative use of the term "the Jews" refers not to all Jews but to the religious leaders, the very ones who so vehemently opposed the fledgling Church.

It's in this context that the words about being the way, the truth and the life must be read. The author of the Gospel is invoking Jesus on his side of the argument against traditional Judaism. The real sense of the passage is then: "You – the Jewish leaders – think you have the truth, but in reality Jesus' teaching alone is the way, the truth and the life." The author gives us not the *actual* words of Jesus but what he believes Jesus would have said in such a situation. It was a bitter family feud and he called on all the trump cards he could muster.

As someone who is trying to be a Christian, the

way for me is Jesus, as he is for all those who aspire to follow him. But, historically, he never claimed to be the *only* way. I believe it would remove an unnecessary stumbling-block to faith and would be a giant step forward if the entire Church could realize this fact and act on it. I like the analogy used by a Native elder I once spoke with. He pointed out that in a tepee, the poles all are separate but converge at the top. So, he said, it is with the "Great Spirit" and the various world faiths.

POURING HOLY WATER ON THE STATUS QUO?

"A barrier that has always held me back from faith in God is the way in which the churches have appeared to be the backbone of both capitalism and militarism. Whenever there's a conflict between faith and patriotism, the latter wins out by such a large margin that the conflict is not even noticed. God appears to be a warrior God, always conservative and a staunch supporter of the status quo."

There is a demonic side to organized religion, a "shadow" in the Jungian sense, which has to be truly faced up to and thoroughly acknowledged. Undoubtedly, ever since the Church's cosy arrangement with the Emperor Constantine in the fourth century, Christianity has often sided with the powers that be and has blessed the status quo in the interests of maintaining or furthering its own privilege and power. It has frequently blessed militarism and the violence of "just wars." You can see ensigns and other military paraphernalia hanging in many major Anglican churches, for example, and on the eve of the Gulf War (Desert Storm), then-president George Bush summoned evangelist Billy Graham to spend the night with him at the White House for comfort and encouragement.

Historically, Karl Marx was right when he said that ruling elites have rejoiced as religion has too often served as the opiate of the masses, promising rewards in an afterlife as the sweetener for enduring the injustices of the present. But, all of this has to do with a distortion of true religion rather than its essence. For proof of this one has only to look at the other side of the coin. There is a prophetic side in all religions that has constantly engaged in a costly and courageous combat with the forces of the status quo. Jesus himself rebuked and overturned all the prevailing values of the society of this time. For a modern example, consider apartheid in South Africa. While it is true that the church of the white minority buttressed and supported this racist doctrine of oppression for many years, some of the bravest and most outspoken opposition to this evil also came from religious sources. We have only to think of leaders like Desmond Tutu, Trevor Huddleston, and a host of others less famous to know that this was so. In Canada today, and indeed around the world, there are coalitions and networks of various faith traditions whose sole aim is to critique and, in many countries, to challenge the political and economic status quo.

One marker of the cost of this witness is the fact that there have been more religious martyrs in this century, particularly in Latin America, than in any other, including the first centuries of the Church.

When we think of Mohandas Gandhi or William Wilberforce, the Wesleys or Bishop Oscar Romero, we can see that religion can be and often has been a force for radical challenge and change. On the issue of war, you have to balance travesties carried out in the name of Christ such as the Crusades with the constant pacifism of the Quakers, the Mennonites and others. I would say to this letter writer and to anyone raised in the Christian tradition: read the prophets, then read the Gospels and the Epistles again. What you will find is not a conformist, conservative, safe or elitist outlook on life. Nor can it be reconciled with any form of violence in the name of God. You cannot take the Sermon on the Mount and especially the Beatitudes, which depict the spiritual qualities of Christianity, seriously, for example, and remain completely at ease in any social order so far known to humanity. In short, we must not allow the historical distortions of true religion committed by any specific denomination, religion or faith to get in the way of a clear vision of the Reality behind them. There is always a tension between true spirituality and any political, economic or social status quo.

Is It Just a Case of Wish Fulfilment?

The following letter from a young woman doing graduate studies in psychology sums up the thrust of several wistful unbelievers who wrote to me:

"My parents were atheists and I grew up without a faith of any kind. I think it would be comforting to believe in God but I have little use for those who use religion as a crutch. It seems to me that the major obstacle to most agnostics or atheists accepting the 'God hypothesis' is the argument of Sigmund Freud and others that God is an illusion, the projection into the skies of a heavenly Father or super-parent."

This is a frequently heard line of reasoning, which seems at first sight to be very plausible. But, however persuasive initially, I believe it withers under further examination. Let's take the religion-as-crutch difficulty first. It is true that many people never give a moment's intellectual concern to matters of faith. They accept blindly and lean heavily! You have already read my opinion about "blind faith," but it's well to consider the fact that crutches have their uses. If you have ever had a broken leg or sustained an injury to a foot, you will know from experience that this is true. By analogy, if there are times when we are limping physically, spiritually or emotionally, we may well use our living faith as a crutch. In these circumstances faith is not something to despise or scorn but to thank God for.

What about the more serious objection, the idea

of belief as a form of wish fulfilment, the projection into the heavens of a needed father figure? Although this writer hasn't talked about the projection of an *indulgent* Parent, so many others have that I must first deal with this notion. The theory would be easier to accept if the concept of God was always and everywhere that of a Parent who indulges our changing demands and whims. But the very reverse is true. The God of the patriarchs and prophets of the Hebrew Bible or Old Testament, the God testified to by Jesus and his apostles, and the vision of God (Allah) professed by Muhammad is not some heavenly mollifier and placator of human foibles. He is more unlike than like us. As theologians would say, he is "wholly other" or transcendent. What's more, this God makes unwelcome and unyielding demands. When the author of the Epistle to the Hebrews writes "for our God is a consuming fire" or that "it is a fearful thing to fall into the hands of the living God," we have left the idea of the cuddly parent in the sky far behind.

Second, and interestingly, the wish-fulfilment or projection argument cuts both ways. I have met many atheists whose profoundest wish is that there be no God. The idea of being in some way responsible to Another who is in and through and above all is deeply repugnant to their own desire to be wholly autonomous and free of any non-human restraint whatever. Freud himself, whose conflict with his own father was never satisfactorily resolved, can be fairly accused of basing his denial of God on precisely the same grounds which he himself uses to attempt to debunk belief. His atheism was, in this view, a form of negative projection or wish fulfilment, a divine absence, the final solution to his father problem.

ECHOES OF CHILDHOOD

A middle-aged woman spoke for many when she wrote:

"My childhood experiences of God were negative and irrelevant. Young as I was, my own inner "spiritual filter" told me that the beliefs I was being taught represented male dominance, greed, war, sexual, social and racial hierarchies and a stifling approach to life. People at church seemed much more concerned with conformity than with true spirituality. Today, when I hear the word 'God,' I cannot let go the embodied mental image that was so dominant in my childhood thoughts. In fact, that's my basic problem with religion today. Emotionally, I can't remove the negative feelings towards the word 'God' developed in my earliest years."

What can I say? First that we need reminding again and again that religion itself is not necessarily the same thing as belief and trust in a Higher Power. The distinction between religion and spirituality is one of the most important points I can make in this discussion of how to find a living faith today. Religion is basically concerned with externals, with rites, dogmas, special buildings, castes of clergy and all the rest. It can have a useful place. But, as a would-be radical Christian, for example, my own belief is that first articulated by the German theologian Dietrich Bonhoeffer, who was convinced that in a deep sense Jesus Christ "came to abolish religion and the need for it altogether." Spirituality, on the other hand, is about the soul or Higher Self and has to do with inner realities and how they are expressed in daily life, especially in our relationships with others. So, I would tell this writer not to worry too much about an inability to reconcile herself with formal "religion."

The problem of bad emotional associations with the word and concept of God, however, is a very prevalent and important concern. Untold damage has been done to millions of people by early experiences where God was represented as a terrifying, despotic, ever-vigilant judge and punisher of wrongdoings real or imagined. The concept of God as a bogey man in the sky runs on the almost unconscious "tapes" of their minds. The remedy is the same as for any other negative emotional traumas suffered in childhood and the later still-formative years. Repression or denial merely compounds the harm done originally. We have to bring the negative concepts or fears up one by one, face them, and replace them with other, more mature and more positive insights. Nothing has the power to drive out bad emotional associations like the force of new understanding and new convictions. Part of the way in which this can be done is by setting aside a time each day for positive considerations about the goodness and love of the Creator God both within us and without. The Bible and other texts can be of great assistance in this.

I know very well from my own experience the truth of what this woman is describing. It's something most people, even the most ardent of believers, have had to cope with. What surprises me – not necessarily about this correspondent – is how so many people outgrow their childish notions of most other areas of life and yet remain at an infantile level when it comes to matters of the spirit. People who would be ashamed not to know what makes a marriage work or how to raise a family are walking around unabashedly with ideas of faith and spirituality garnered in Sunday School or its equivalent. If we are indeed spiritual beings, as I believe, if there is a world of the spirit and of Spirit, it is the most important aspect of our existence. It behooves us to treat it with the utmost seriousness. This is what Jesus was really talking about when he said: "Seek first the Kingdom of God; all the rest will then fall into place." When the search for God is in earnest, we soon find we are able, little by little, to "put away childish things." Consider this little story:

A young man who was convinced he had a great hunger for God came to a distinguished guru in India for assistance. He hung around the ashram and pestered the guru for many days wanting to know the secret of finding God. Finally, one day the guru told the youth to accompany him down to the nearby river. He waded out into the water until he was waist-deep and called the young man to join him. When he did, the guru told him he was going to dip him into the water in a kind of baptism. The young man was agreeable and submerged himself while the guru supported him. To his dismay, however, he felt the guru's powerful hands suddenly grip him and hold him there. He struggled to get his head out but to no avail. Finally, after what seemed like an eternity, the hold was relaxed and he emerged coughing and spitting – and very angry. The guru looked at him for a moment and then said: "When you really want to know God as much as you wanted air a few moments ago, then you will find him. You won't need a guru to tell you the way."

WHERE TO START?

"In answer to your request for letters from wistful unbelievers, I'm writing to say I count myself as one of that company. I'm looking forward to retirement shortly (I'm an investment analyst) in the hopes of devoting more time to what Thomas Moore calls the Care of the Soul. My chief difficulty is knowing where to start."

I want to try to answer this most important query with a kind of meditation in praise of stillness: I was passing through London once on an assignment elsewhere for the *Toronto Star*. I decided to use the time to try to arrange an interview with the Archbishop of

Canterbury at the time, the Most Rev. Michael Ramsey. Many will remember him: the quintessential archbishop with longish white hair flowing from a dignified bald dome, a great craggy brow with fiercely thick eyebrows, and yet a face like a cherub. I had long admired his intellect and his wisdom both in his books and in his public statements. It turned out that at the time he was involved in meetings at Brompton Oratory, so I hailed a cab and arrived there during a break for refreshments. Descending to the church basement with my trenchcoat still on I spotted Ramsey sitting at a table by himself with a teacup in front of him. Weaving through the crowd I began to introduce myself. But before I could say anything very much, he picked up the cup and saucer. "How very kind of you," he said. "The tea urn is over there." So, I went and got him a refill and, just as he gave me a nod of dismissal, managed to blurt out that I was a Canadian journalist and wanted to arrange an interview. His eyes twinkled and he said: "Don't count on it; don't count on it." That was it. His mind was elsewhere and my plans had to wait. Calls to his office next day proved to no avail. Eventually though, on another trip, I did manage to talk to him. One thing he said stands out above the rest. Asked what he considered his major achievement he said: "I think I have mastered the art of doing nothing." Aware of his books, his work and his busy life, I knew he didn't mean this in the sense of laziness or simply passing the time. He was talking about the art of creative, meditative sitting or being still. That was why, when called upon, he always had something significant to say. I must add that in compelling me to wait both on him and for him, he taught me something about humility and patience, as well.

It is as well to remember that most of the truly creative leaps in history began when the innovators were "doing nothing." This is true of scientific breakthroughs – Isaac Newton under the apple tree, Archimedes in his bath, Einstein sitting on a streetcar, and so on, endlessly. It is true in the spiritual realm too – Jesus in the wilderness before his ministry began, Paul's vision while simply walking to Damascus, St. Augustine while meditating in a garden, Buddha sitting under a bo tree, or Muhammad praying in the mountain cave.

Some of the best books have been written when stillness and "doing nothing" were forced on the authors. Consider how many have been forged and completed in prison. John Bunyan's *Pilgrim's Progress* is an obvious example, but there have been scores of others, including parts of the New Testament, and, in the modern era, the letters of the German theologian and anti-Nazi Dietrich Bonhoeffer. Viktor Frankl's moving book *Man's Search for Meaning* was conceived and written amidst the horror of a Nazi concentration camp. The late Bishop John Robinson once told me he wrote his best-known and most controversial book, *Honest to God*, in 1962 when he was hospitalized for several weeks with a complex leg injury. Every experienced farmer knows that the truly fertile field is one that regularly is allowed to lie fallow for a while "doing nothing."

Many people today, like the above letter writer, are searching for God. They run to this preacher or that guru, following the noise of the crowd and the slogans with the cleverest spin. But the reality itself still eludes them. There's a marvellous story in I Kings 19 that speaks to this condition. Elijah the prophet had reached a low point in his life, so bad in fact that he prayed for death. He was being hunted down by Queen Jezebel, there was rampant apostasy and idolatry all around him, and he felt utterly defeated and alone. God, too, he felt had forsaken him. He went into the wilderness and, while he lay in a depressed and anxious sleep, "an angel touched him." He was told to make a journey to a cave on Mount Sinai. There, alone in that lunar-like remoteness, God gave him a fresh revelation. First there was a wind strong enough to break rocks into pieces. "But the Lord was not in the wind." Then there was an earthquake followed by a consuming fire. But God was not in these either. Finally after all the noise and spectacle there was "a still, small voice," the assurance of the Divine Presence with him and within. Incidentally, whereas he thought, like some people today, that he was the only one who stood for what was ethical and true, he was told there were "seven thousand left in Israel" who had not "bowed unto Baal."

In the West today, with its urban cacophony and media bombardment, there is lots more leisure time but little real quietness. There are many who either from circumstances beyond their control or by choice have a lot of time to do nothing. Yet, they have no notion of true stillness. We need to be reminded that the most basic of all prayers is "Lord, teach me to be still." Prayer is conversation with God. Too often the communication is all one way as we recite our needs. But it is in the stillness, if we listen, that we hear the voice of God. My advice to this correspondent, then, and to all who echo his question, is to begin with a regular time of quiet. You can call it meditation but no special mantras and postures are needed. Personally, as I have indicated already, I find walking in the open country or along some rural byway just as conducive to the kind of stillness required as any traditional discipline. The important thing is to find what works for you. Be still. Be open. Ask for God's presence and guidance. It will come.

The Role of Feelings

"I am a forty-five-year-old professional writer who has tried all her life to believe in God. I have tried as well to make it a matter of deep commitment, but often – sometimes for very long periods – I feel nothing, no sense of any presence, no awareness of any reality in praying or worship. Shouldn't there be more?"

In living a life of faith we all need to be reminded:

don't expect to have ecstatic revelations or some warm, fuzzy feeling of God's presence overwhelm you. I received a letter recently from one of the most energetic and keen Christian leaders I have ever known. He was writing to thank me for something I had written on the use of stillness in one's spiritual life. He had been going through a difficult time and feeling some discouragement. Reading between the lines, though, it was clear to me he had been experiencing a phenomenon that people of all faiths who are sincere seekers sooner or later – and some quite frequently – come to know intimately. The mystics call it the "dark night of the soul." In its milder forms it is best described as a period of dryness. It feels like the absence of God. It can be very intense. Prayers seem to mock one, bouncing back as it were from the ceiling. Some have described this aspect of it by saying "the heavens themselves seem made of brass." Or, our spirit becomes so lethargic and confused that we are unable to pray at all. It can be reassuring to know that no matter how saintly or spiritual some people are, no matter how fervently they talk about "knowing the Lord" or living the abundant life, they too have times when there is a void within. God, as the Psalmist says, seems to "hide His face" and to be deaf to all entreaties. Instead of enjoying the divine Presence, one faces emptiness, the divine absence. The garden becomes a desert. It is easy to falter.

Before we jump to the conclusion that our faith is a mirage or that there is some ethical or deep spiritual problem blocking the Spirit's flow, in these circumstances, we should look first at more practical matters. As a parson, and later as a seminary teacher, I often had students and others come for counselling about a supposed spiritual difficulty erasing their sense of God's reality only to find that what they really needed was to find a way of safely venting some repressed rage; to get some vigorous physical exercise; to lighten up a bit about everything, including religion; find somebody they could help in some way – or whatever. I used to tell my students that every parsonage should have a punching-bag hung in the cellar. Then, after a frustrating meeting or a tough encounter with a parishioner, the minister could go down and vent his or her feelings. There'd be less depression among clergy if they did this.

But, no matter how healthy we are or how good our relationships with others may be, living a life of faith in God is no guarantee of sensing a perpetual oneness with and joy in the Creator. In fact, while it's wonderful to have exalted emotions, and even perhaps occasional ecstasy, travelling a spiritual path is not really a matter of feelings at all. It's a commitment of mind and will as well as of the heart. We believe because we have come to know our belief to be true. We stay obedient to our belief through good feelings and bad because we *will* ourselves to remain true to the One who has promised to be faithful forever. The only effective way to deal with dryness or times of God's apparent absence is to keep at our post, remembering both God's promises and past goodness – "until the night is gone." The shortest way out of this particular kind of wilderness is to sit down and be still – and listen – within it, and then go straight through.

What I, and many others, have experienced, however, is that there is a paradoxical element in this process. The time of absence or of spiritual dryness often is seen, in retrospect, to have been the place where God's Presence was most clearly at work in our lives. One way of putting it is to say that when it comes to spiritual growth we learn far more and advance further during or just after the bleak periods than we do in the halcyon days when we are more or less on top of the world. God is not playing games with us. There is never a time when we are beyond his care and love. But we have a desperate need to become more mature, more fully what we are designed to be, and that doesn't come by singing and dancing one's way through life.

I do not believe the loving Intelligence we call God ever sends grief, illness or spiritual dryness to do us good. (The idea that evil is sent that good may come is immoral, a version of the end justifying the means). Rather, bad times are simply a fact of life. But, properly understood and used they can nourish us for the road ahead. In short, what we all-too-human believers often experience as God's absence is really but a different modality or dimension of the Presence. By perseverance and trust we can find ourselves saying of any particular dry spell what Jacob said of a similar experience long ago. Remember the time when, having cheated his brother, Esau, twice, he was being hunted and was on the run. He found himself alone, in the dark, in the bare wilderness. Frightened and cold, he lay down with only a rock for a pillow. Then he had his famous dream of the ladder going up to heaven with angels ascending and descending it. Later, he awoke and said with great surprise: "Surely God was in this place and I knew it not!" This is a key biblical dream and I will return to it later.

THE WORD OF GOD?

"The Bible as the Word of 'God' lacks credibility. The Bible is indeed a wonderful book but how can one accept the writings when they were not written until some years after the fact and in some cases close to a hundred years? My own experience is that even things written a day after are subject to misinterpretation. The writings would be subject to prejudices of the author and would be distorted to enhance the Christian religion as a movement."

This young man speaks for many people today. Most holy books claim to be inspired and to be the Word of God. What I have to say in reference to his specific citation of the Bible applies in general outline to the Qur'an, the Bhagavad-Gita, the Upanishads, and all other sacred texts. The declaration that "this is God's infallible word" is the watchword of Christian fundamentalism. When you ask a fundamentalist, "Why should I believe it's God's Word?" their answer is, "Because that's what it claims to be." This, of course, is the circular, dog-chasing-its-tail logic that is no logic at all.

I already stated in Chapter 2 my own high regard of the Bible. It falls, however, far short of any fundamentalist, literalist approach. Before going further, however, let me give one word of caution. We live in a time when info-glut is a huge obstacle to our clear remembrance of anything, and we often fail to recognize the tremendous memory powers of people living mainly with oral tradition. The Polynesians, for example, can remember genealogies stretching back over centuries. In the fourth century, John Chrysostom lived in a cave alone for three years and memorized the entire Bible – both Testaments! This doesn't mean I want to argue that the early disciples of Jesus had perfect memories or that the Gospel writers, for example, didn't editorialize or take liberties with the tradition. They did. I simply want to put the problem of the Gospels being written well after the fact in its proper cultural perspective. When Paul in I Corinthians says he handed on to his followers the same tradition that was given to him by the other apostles, he uses a precise, technical Greek term (*paradidomai*) for the careful handling of an oral tradition. This commands scholarly respect.

Yet, after having studied the Bible for years, and having taught the New Testament professionally for seven years, I can say without fear of contradiction that there are, as this letter writer believes, errors, misunderstandings and signs of cultural prejudices in the Bible. The first Gospel to be written, Mark, dates to about 65 A.D. This is approximately thirty years after the events it describes. Its chronology is extremely sketchy and the actual teachings of Jesus outlined in it are scant when compared, say, with the Gospel of Matthew, which was written about 85 A.D. In *For Christ's Sake* I have written about how the picture of Jesus in the Gospels was enhanced. The problem of sorting out the Jesus of history from the Christ of faith is well known.

Each Gospel writer has his own theology and hence his own special interests. For example, if you didn't know the author of Matthew was a Jew and that his Gospel reflects a time of bitter conflict between the emerging Church and the synagogue, you'd be justified in thinking the entire document was anti-Semitic. Its denunciations of the Pharisees, who were the Jewish leaders of Matthew's day, are biting. Words are undoubtedly put into the mouth of Jesus – "You generation of vipers," "whited sepulchres" – which the historical Jesus never spoke. John's gospel as we have already seen is widely recognized as more of a spiritual meditation on the Christ Event than an attempt to give a historical, biographical account. When you come to St. Paul, it is evident that his own personality and biases are imprinted on every page of his letters. He even tells us on occasion that on certain specific subjects he is giving us his own opinion rather than some word from above. He has no problem with sending a runaway slave, Onesimus, back to his owner. He orders women to wear veils in assembling for worship and bids them to keep silent as well. His view of marriage and the family is unabashedly patriarchal. His views of sex are generally seen as being negative, although on this point he has been greatly misunderstood. That, however, is a discussion for another time.

The point I want to underscore is that all scriptures are mediated and composed by human beings. Consequently, they bear the marks of that humanity – its strengths and its shortcomings. Nobody, even the holiest of persons, is culturally neutral. God doesn't engage in automatic writing or play on the human author like a flute or other musical instrument. That is to say, the author is not a passive, mechanical transmitter of a pure, spiritual message, and for this reason we should never give absolute or divine status to any sacred literary text. We humans long for infallibility and for absolute certainty. But, to claim it for any book is to indulge in idolatry. The problem with the Protestant Reformation, for example, is that it rejected the idolatry of certain doctrines of the Mass and of papal authority and took up bibliolatry – the worship of a book, the Bible – instead.

The Bible and other sacred texts are not God, nor are they his completely unmediated word or mind.

But, they all in some way – and, for me, particularly the Bible – contain tracks or clues which lead to him. As a friend of mine has put it: deer tracks are not the same thing as the deer itself. But, if you want to encounter a deer, it's not a bad idea to look where others have found the tracks and then have seen the deer. Sacred books tell of the encounter with God of other humans very much like us. They point to where and how we can have a similar encounter ourselves.

WHY WORSHIP?

"If there is a 'God,' why would he want or need us to worship him? Certainly he should be respected and his leadership followed, but why worship? If he does want us to worship him, should we not therefore live the lives of monks?"

That letter was from a middle-aged man. The following excerpt makes the same point. The writer is a married woman with two sons raised "with no faith":

"Why is it God needs so much praise? A little respect, yes – I like my children to treat me with some courtesy. But I certainly don't envision a future in which they will have to be on their hands and knees to me every day just because I gave birth to them and raised them. Yet, we are told, God requires this kind of fawning attention from us. . . . I've met some pretty dreadful God-fawners!"

This question is one that troubled me deeply at one point in my student days at Oriel College, Oxford. My philosophy tutor, Richard Robinson, now in his nineties and long retired, was an outspoken atheist. He had little use for the idea of a deity so insecure and concerned about his glory that he needed to be told how great he was day in and day out. It caused me a lot of thought. The chief misunderstanding lies, I believe, in taking certain passages in the Bible much too literally. As the human book it is, it often puts into the mouth of God the limited thinking of those trying their best to describe his will and ways. I don't believe any God worthy of the name either needs or covets our constant worship. But, suppose the very opposite is true. Suppose the Creator has made us to need to worship, to need to give our ultimate allegiance to something or Someone. Suppose that in his infinite wisdom he knows that while he has no need of our worship we have a desperate need to express it towards the Ground of our very being.

It helps if we understand the root meaning of the word worship. Literally, it means worth-ship, the giving of value or worth to something. As humans, we have a deep need to ascribe worth to various aspects of our lives – to life itself, to friends, to love and family, to work, possessions, hobbies, the environment, and on and on. It makes a profound difference to the kind of people we are and the kind of relationships we have if we give our ultimate worth-ship or worship to secondary things, to money, success, sex or whatever. Communist societies, for example, are governed and conditioned by the giving of ultimate value to the state itself. People in materialistic societies may say they worship God, but in actual fact they worship the bottom line on financial statements and its results. As Jesus said, where your treasure (worship) is, there will your heart (spirit) be also. We need to worship God because, if we do not, we end up worshipping some false god. Western society today is strewn with many bogus deities commanding total allegiance and devotion. It can be celebrity, it can be professional sports, money, the myth of perpetual youth, work, technology. But, whatever it is, it leaves in us a sense of emptiness and alienation. The human heart is hungry for the God beyond all idols.

There is another aspect to worshipping God other than our sheer need for it. There are times – by no means confined to religious occasions or sacred buildings; indeed most often quite outside them – when our searching soul is simply overwhelmed by the vision or sense of God's goodness and grace. It can come through some piece of music, some sharing of intimacy, or the experience of nature's beauty and complexity. In these moments, we are filled with an overpowering sense of gratitude and of awe. Worship, be it as simple as an inarticulate prayer or a sense of inner peace in that Presence, is the most natural and fitting response we can make. It is in the act of worship, either a specific response or the direction and goal espoused by the whole of one's life, that the soul finds its own true worth and meaning.

Regarding the logic of becoming monks to fulfil our need to worship, it may well make sense for a few. But, the view of worship as chanting, praying and asceticism of various kinds is overly narrow. Life is worship properly understood. It encompasses our outlook and approach to everything we do or say no matter how "secular" our calling and vocation may be. You can worship God in front of your computer or in your kitchen by keeping a sense of his presence at all times. You don't need to retreat from this world in order to be in touch with and guided by the world of Spirit which penetrates it on every side.

LIFE AFTER DEATH?

"In my religious upbringing, life after death was portrayed in terms of a flesh-and-bones resurrection some day in the future. We were told we would go to 'heaven' if we lived a good life and would sit around all day talking to our relatives under the careful ordering of a benevolent Figure. If we lived a bad life, we went to 'hell.' Surely if there is such a thing as life after death it can only be in a spirit form and one not recognizable to us in our earthly condition."

Over the years, I have had hundreds of letters from people who are troubled by the teaching of the major religions that there is life in another dimension after death. My invitation to my column readers to write of their problems in coming to faith in God not surprisingly produced another spate of correspondence on this theme. Few things, I'm convinced, have been more off-putting to wistful non-believers than the sometimes quite bizarre religious language and concepts surrounding this topic. Indeed, that was the main reason I spent three years researching the whole body of beliefs about a life to come for my book *Life After Death*.

I cannot begin to reproduce even a summary of that work here. Suffice it to say that, while coming to the firm conclusion that the weight of evidence lies heavily on the probability of an existence beyond the grave, I found most of the traditional thinking and terminology sadly wanting. For example, I discovered that the doctrine of a hell of fiery, eternal punishment is not the teaching of either Jesus or Paul, his greatest convert. The Church's insistence on it through the ages has had more to do with its desire for control than with proclaiming an abundant life. It is an idea that has caused an incalculable amount of suffering and harm here and now for millions of people.

Similarly, I found that traditional views of heaven, with gates of gold and all that milk and honey, are a caricature of what is really intended by sacred texts. I believe that the life to come is not about sitting around or about endless choral efforts punctuated by the occasional sermon. It's a continuing progression of growing and learning – a further evolution of the soul. Certainly we are not going to have flesh-and-blood bodies in any future state. As Paul says, there is a physical body and there is a spiritual body. We will not be disembodied spirits, but have the kind of body suited to an entirely new dimension of being. If this kind of thinking boggles your mind, I suggest a light reading course in modern physics. As an alternative to that, the part of my book *Life After Death* that has attracted the most favourable comments from readers is the chapter "New Light from Science," which deals with this aspect.

In sum, when it comes to this – and other subjects of profound concern – my advice to the honest seeker is to disregard the popularly held religious jargon surrounding the issue and struggle for yourself with the core of the matter. If what is popularly and traditionally believed to be Christianity is what it is really all about then I ceased being a Christian in that sense at least thirty years ago. Thankfully, as already indicated, a living spirituality and a relationship with the Divine Ground of our being have very little to do with dogmatic religion, whether Christian or any other.

The Hypocrisy of Religion and Religionists

Not surprisingly, many readers wrote to say they are deeply troubled and put off by the hypocrisy of much that is said and done in the name of God and religion. Here are two brief excerpts which make the point:

"As a son of the manse (now a practising psychologist), I have been utterly disappointed with the hypocrisies,

legalism and sterility of ecclesiastical religion which seems so long on fellowship but so short on true faith."

"There are those who point to the change God has wrought in their lives as proof that he exists and cares. I have trouble with this. I see very little evidence to suggest that the devout are any better than non-believers – and indeed, many of the devout spend a great deal of time admitting they are sinners (even though they strangely want the rest of us to believe at the same time that they are still better than non-believers!) My own mother had a born-again experience. According to her it totally changed her life . . . but I saw absolutely no difference in her as a result; her parenting certainly didn't change. Today she is still insecure, self-absorbed."

I am sure most of us could also wax eloquent on this subject. The hypocrisies of the devout and of the institutions that nourish them are endless – a very safe and all-too-easy target for any critic. I don't hold for a moment that they should in any way be played down, ignored or excused. Part of my function as a writer and commentator on religion over the years has been to highlight religious hypocrisy whenever possible – a most unpopular stance, I must add. However, the cause of truth and the ultimate good of organized religion itself demand this of any religion writer who takes the role seriously.

It's easy to criticize hypocrites, but to allow them to stand in the way of one's own spiritual quest and one's soul-commitment to God is, to put it bluntly, a feeble – even stupid – mistake. The fact that there are counterfeiters who circulate bogus fifty- or hundred-dollar bills has never stopped anyone I know from accepting or using money in their daily lives. In fact, there would never be even a possibility of counterfeit money if it weren't for the existence of real money out there. Religious hypocrisy would never dare so much as to raise its ugly head were it not for the fact that there is indeed genuine spirituality and true religion around for it to mimic or pretend to. What is more, being human, we all – believers and non-believers alike – are prone to self-deception and to the practice of presenting a face to the world that does not necessarily mirror our true selves. We all have to guard against the hypocrisy of seeing the hypocrisy of others while missing our own.

But, ultimately, we cannot let the failure of others, as well as our own failures, in living up to the levels of faith professed weaken or abort our trust in the Ultimate Source of our lives. There is far too much at stake for such a flimsy ploy! See the hypocrisies clearly, both your own and those of the avowedly pious, and resolve to be and do better. The real challenge to each of us is this: become what you really are and what you were meant to be, a mature Child of God.

Meaningless Creeds?

A number of people who have been raised in the Christian faith wrote about the difficulty of accepting the historic creeds. Because of them, they said, any kind of faith in God now seems difficult if not impossible. Here is one example, from a seventy-one-year-old man who says he finds himself increasingly lonely. He feels he can't share his doubts with other family members who still seem to find church-going meaningful for fear of destroying their faith. His wife adds to his burden by telling him to keep his doubts to himself:

"While all our family have been and are active church-goers – one brother-in-law was a minister of the United Church of Canada – I have been plagued with doubts since my early twenties. A lot of things bother me, including the hypocrisies of the TV evangelists, but my chief problem lies with the creeds we were taught and which are still recited every Sunday in most churches. Most of what they state so certainly seems like mumbo jumbo to me."

Here is the beginning, at least, of an answer:

A man I knew, now deceased, was a devout churchman all his life. He served the Church in many ways, including several terms as rector's warden, the highest lay function in an Anglican parish. Noticing how he always stood stiffly at attention during the recital of the creed, I once asked him whether or not he really understood its meaning. He thought for a moment and said somewhat ruefully: "I'll be damned if I do!" Sadly, he represents a vast company of people. As I wrote recently in one of my weekly newspaper columns: "Everywhere people are searching for God and instead are offered hoary, virtually incomprehensible creeds with the hand of death upon them." Since writing that, I have been pilloried by some and praised by others. One interesting response came from a reader who asked: "Given your own somewhat liberal convictions, how do you manage to say the Creed yourself in church?" A short answer is, "With very great difficulty."

The truth is I identify most with a remark once made many years ago by that great Christian apologist, the late Bishop Stephen Neill. Speaking at a mission he held in the University of Toronto's Convocation Hall, Neill said there were times when the only part of the Creed he felt really sure of was the phrase, "And was crucified under Pontius Pilate." The rest is the language of faith and, even more importantly, of metaphor and symbolism. I recite the Creed when I attend church – fully aware that almost none of it can be taken literally – mostly out of a desire to identify with the continuity and tradition it symbolizes. For any modern believer who wrestles with the intellectual and moral issues conjured up by faith today, the Nicene Creed, common to all of the historic denominations, presents some enormous problems. The major one is that it was formulated in the fourth century in a crucible of power politics and in terms of Greek philosophy and reflects the worldview of that day – one in which, for example, heaven was up, hell was down, and earth lay in between. Thus, it says that Christ "came down from heaven," and he "ascended into heaven."

According to this creed, he now "sitteth on the right hand of the Father."

No matter how fervent one's faith, to take any of that literally is to misunderstand it grossly. We know now that there is a minimum of forty billion galaxies in the visible universe, which makes the idea of any three-decker reality ludicrous. What's more, God does not have a right hand at which Christ, like some potentate at the court of the Emperor Constantine, can actually sit. Constantine, of course, had called for the Council of Nicea itself in 325 A.D. The Creed gets its name from the place and, in this instance, takes its metaphor from Constantine's imperial court. His real concern was unity for his empire. Even when your understanding of the Creed allows such nuances, there are major stumbling-blocks. You have to be aware that, in spite of the phrase "the *Father* Almighty," God is beyond gender. Nor does God literally beget sons. The language about "the only-begotten Son of God, Begotten of the Father before all worlds . . . Begotten, not made" is entirely metaphorical and must of necessity be so. The recent politically correct translation of the New Testament and Psalms by Oxford University Press (1995) escapes the gender problem of "son" by calling Jesus God's "child." But the difficult metaphor of God's offspring remains.

The central statement "And [He] was incarnate by the Holy Ghost of the Virgin Mary" must also be understood as the language of myth; not of fairy tales, but of religious myth, which uses imagery and metaphor to convey truths that cannot be communicated otherwise. In *For Christ's Sake* I set out (as Bishop John Spong and many others have also done) the reasons for questioning the absolute divinity of Jesus and for not taking the Virgin Birth as literal, historical fact. It's not that I don't believe God couldn't but that he didn't break the natural laws of the universe at this point. Jesus was fully human. In other words, he had a human father as well as a human mother. Those who were said to have had virgin births in antiquity – and there were many – were not thought of as human but as demi-gods. Paul, whose letters were written earlier than the Gospels, says nothing about the Virgin Birth. The later stories of the birth of Jesus (found only in Matthew and Luke) were simply trying to emphasize the unique importance of his person and teaching. The spiritual meaning of this doctrine is what is of paramount significance. In a sense each of us must have a virgin birth, a waking to our own spiritual nature as also the "children" of God.

The historic creeds of Christianity should not, in my opinion, be shelved or thrown out. They need to be reinterpreted. But, in addition, the Church needs to fashion new, much more open formulae of faith to which we can assent without first having to commit intellectual suicide. We are not necessarily smarter than those who wrote the Nicene Creed, but we do live in vastly different times. Not to recognize this is to fail God as well as our own generation.

DOES GOD HATE WOMEN?

Next to the problem of pain, suffering and evil (I have kept that for a chapter on its own because no other issue attracted as much attention from respondents), the most frequently cited difficulty in having faith was the teachings and attitudes of organized religions down the centuries towards women. I can only give a brief sampling of some of those letters here:

"I was raised as a Roman Catholic and for many years practised and believed. However, when I became an adult female I could no longer follow the Church's doctrines, finding them patriarchal and especially cruel and oppressive to its women followers. Then, after the horrid events of the Mt. Cashel orphanage scandal and stories of sexual abuse of young boys elsewhere by priests and brothers I felt a terrible loss of faith and hope in religion in general."

A woman who was raised as a Baptist in rural Alberta wrote of the strictness of the church of her childhood – no playing cards, no makeup or jewellery, no dancing, no alcohol – and yet she was personally aware of "children who were regularly beaten senseless by their fathers. However, this kind of abuse was never considered wrong." Eventually, as an adult, she found her way to feminist literature:

"When I began reading feminist theory, I could scarcely believe the opprobrium and hatred directed towards women by the Church Fathers. The scales fell quickly from my eyes and I am convinced that Christianity can never be reconciled with feminism. By cursing Eve rather than blessing her for her child-bearing ability, the Christian God becomes an enemy of all women. What do I believe now?

I'm not sure that I need to believe anything. I do have a closer connection with my own nature and am more aware than ever before of the sky, the stars, the trees and the changing seasons."

These final two excerpts are typical of dozens of other women who wrote to me in a similar vein:

"I don't have an extensive knowledge of the major faiths, including my own Eastern orthodoxy. But I resent deeply their lack of regard and treatment of women. I have been left with a strong impression that religion is another male creation designed to subordinate and oppress women."

"I have a major problem in finding a vital faith. It's one that comes from within the Church itself. It has resulted in my complete withdrawal from the Anglican Church in which I was raised because of its patriarchal structures and its utter failure to consider the spiritual and even the physical well-being of women. I tried for a long time to work within the structure but failed. I'm female and sixty years old."

Many of the letters on this theme were extremely painful to read. The honesty and the sharp sense of hurt and betrayal were palpable on every page. It is a colossal irony that women, the majority of whom are by nature and instinct so much more spiritual than men – perhaps because of their more intimate connection with the deepest processes of nature itself through child-bearing, or perhaps because they are simply more open to their intuitive side – should have been for centuries the victims of so much heavy-handed, unjust suppression and oppression by all the major faiths. It is true that there has been an enormous amount of consciousness-raising about this in the past twenty years or so. But, as I have tried to stress in my columns and some of my books, for millions of women it is all too little and too late. Indeed, one of the most striking features of the current decline in church attendance in the Western world is the high rate of exodus by well-educated women.

There is absolutely no question that whatever the original intentions and attitudes of the founders of the various faiths may have been – and in spite of many notable achievements on behalf of women by specific religious groups at different times – the traditional religions of Judaism, Christianity, and Islam still discriminate against women today. There is no doubt either but that at a very deep level all of us have been taught and inculturated to believe that God is male. This is an obvious caricature of the truth, a piece of theological nonsense, yet at a visceral point the distortion lurks on still with real potency to do harm.

I would be the last person to suggest to women who feel as these writers do that they should return to their church or denomination or even that they should try attending some more enlightened religious body. As I have said before, the issue here is not one of belonging to this faith community or that. As Jesus once said, there comes a time to "let the dead bury their dead." Part of a rebirth of true faith today may well be the decision by more and more women to forsake the dry bones of "religion" in order to rediscover God. It may help to address God as she. At the very least, the female pronoun serves to remind us all of God as a loving, nurturing Creator.

My own belief is that all the dissatisfaction, unrest and even chaos among thinking women today over the matter of religion is a sign that the spiritual reality we call God is saying something to us. Both the planet and the human beings on it need healing as never before. I believe women will lead the way in this healing – led themselves, whether they are conscious of it or not, by the Spirit of God. Many women will no doubt feel called to remain and to continue to struggle within the religious institutions that have nurtured them, however badly. Their witness is needed there too. But, the real step ahead will come, I'm convinced, from the "diaspora" who have left their past orthodoxies behind and who are willing, in spite of massive doubts, to open themselves to new spiritual insights and experiences. They may well not need the old, formal religion. However, like all humanity they "live and move and have their being" in God every moment of every day. My suggestion to each is to open herself to this and then see where it (God) leads. I am certain a fresh spiritual awakening is under way as we prepare to enter the third millennium A.D., and I am just as certain that women are destined to be in the vanguard.

4

The Power of Evil

When I first invited readers of my newspaper column to write to me regarding obstacles to a committed belief, I knew, of course, that many would mention the problem of pain and suffering and evil in general. I was not prepared, however, for the outpouring that followed. More than half of the roughly two hundred letters I received were concerned chiefly with this problem. The survey, of course, was by no means a scientific sampling. Yet it does suggest that no other single issue is as big a stumbling-block to faith for modern men and women as this one. The letters were remarkable for their seriousness, their compassion and their honest sense of bewilderment at the idea that a loving God could or would permit such injustice and cruelty in the world he is alleged to have made.

It is impossible to do full justice to the thought and feelings which went into the composition of these letters. But, the following snippets give the reader at least an indication of their overall tone and thrust.

A woman who called herself an agnostic and is "grateful" to be alive in such a wonderful cosmos wrote:

"I would like to know how the theologians explain why a Creator could set up such a cruel plan for living creatures. Suffering and agony are intrinsic to the evolutionary process. The balance depends on one animal eating another. The weakest bird gets shoved from the nest. The cat 'tortures' the mouse."

A young businessman who thinks Freud's idea of religion as wish fulfilment is the only thing that makes sense, given the problem of evil, wrote:

"Awareness of human suffering overwhelms any idea of providential design in the cosmos. Consider a child who is mortally injured, sick or starving. Consider that many such children don't even have parents to console them in their agony. One just has to watch the news to see that such suffering is multiplied a millionfold every day. Can anyone higher than the crocodile on the scale of sensitivity fail to be tortured by this suffering, or frustrated by the knowledge that no amount of good will will completely stop it?"

A woman who attends the Unity Church, and says she wishes she could have the childlike faith many of her friends there have, wrote:

"I want to believe so much . . . and at times it seems that it is almost there; but I cannot reconcile the earthquakes,

violence, hatred and all the other evils that are so prevalent in this world with a loving God."

Her thought was echoed by another, younger woman:

"*I cannot reconcile a God who is good yet allows child or animal abuse. A baby or an animal cannot defend itself and it suffers so much pain, i.e., broken legs, ribs, starvation, etc.*"

A woman who has left the Catholicism in which she was raised wrote to say she finds "the relative stability of atheism" preferable to "the relentless upheavals of faith." The upheavals she cites are due to the difficulty we are now discussing – trying to believe in a loving God in the face of all that contradicts that belief:

"*This world is full of cruelty, evil and senseless pain. I find this logically impossible to reconcile with the notion of a divine power for good; and recently I have begun to see that trying to believe in a good God is like knowingly embarking on a dysfunctional relationship: i.e., one characterized by a lack of predictability, unspoken hurts, and a neverending attempt to smooth things over so that the horror will remain hidden inside. It's the trying to see God in the meaninglessness that tears your soul apart.*"

One reader, who didn't sign her name, simply sent a sheet of pictures of children who have died as the result of accidents, crimes or disease. There were newspaper cutlines explaining the nature of the tragedy in each case and an overall hand-printed heading that said: "More proof that 'God' has neither mercy nor love for humans!"

Finally, and quite arbitrarily, because there was so much more, I offer you this passage from a letter from a middle-aged man:

"If such a Being as God ever existed, He/She has obviously died or is asleep at the switch. Surely no living, awake, omnipotent, and loving God could ever permit the suffering of innocents which has prevailed throughout recorded history and which seemingly increases daily. Pursuing a faith in any Being so stupid or careless as to create and permit the spread of humanity as we know it seems a pointless and ultimately destructive route to follow."

It is true that pain and loss are always with us and that the list of plagues, catastrophes and senseless tortures and slaughters is virtually endless. One can barely read the daily newspaper without being stirred both to rage and grief. In my own lifetime there has been the horror of Hitler's concentration camps and the murder of six million Jews. Just as many people died under the virulent regime of Pol Pot in Cambodia. There is the more recent wanton killing of about one million people in bloody Rwanda, and the atrocities being committed even as I write this by Russian soldiers against the Chechens. Women and children have been massacred. Just a few months ago, some unknown right-wing terrorists blew up the federal building in Oklahoma City, killing about 170 people, including nearly twenty small children in the day-care centre. Sometimes it seems the only cry going up from the earth is one of massive pain from humans and from animals as well. Small wonder that for humans this cry is accompanied by the roaring of an agonized "why?"

A LOVING GOD OR A DIVINE SADIST?

Disappointing as it may seem at first thought, the ultimate response to what St. Paul once called this "mystery of evil" is a humble and quite candid one. We don't know why evil exists. The best minds in the world – while I have read most of what has been said down the centuries on this subject, I don't pretend to have read or to know it all – have wrestled with this question. From the Book of Job to Carl Jung's book *The Answer to Job*, and from C. S. Lewis's *The Problem of Pain* to Rabbi Kushner's best-seller, *When Bad Things Happen to Good People*, the problem of pain, suffering and evil has been raised and dissected again and again. Yet, however noble and inspiring all this literature is, the question of how there can be a loving God and an unending litany of disasters, undeserved personal tragedies and suffering of the innocent has never been answered to the complete satisfaction of our hearts or intellects.

I can only relate here what makes the most, though admittedly partial and provisional, sense to me. Before doing that, however, I need to make one other point. For the unbeliever, the person who believes this is all there is, who is convinced we are alone in the universe and in our grief, for the one who thinks the cosmos has merely thrown us up by chance, there is no intellectual problem. His or her explanation of evil is: "That is just how it is." Their suffering, of course, is just as keen, but they do not have the added, enormous mental and moral anguish, alluded to by one of my letter writers above, of trying to reconcile two seemingly contradictory ideas – a benevolent Creator and a pain-wracked world. They talk about believers using a "crutch" or taking the easy way when, because of this issue, holding a reasonable faith is the infinitely harder road. Theodicy (how to justify the ways of God for human beings) is a problem only when you first of all believe in a God of justice, love and mercy.

Having said that, let us begin. The traditional Christian explanation for the existence of evil is based upon the Genesis story of the Fall. Adam and Eve sinned by disobediently eating the fruit of a forbidden tree, in the middle of the Garden of Eden. As a result, they were banished from the garden and cursed, together with all their subsequent progeny, with the punishment of suffering and death. The very ground or earth itself was cursed as well. "Cursed is the ground for thy sake; in sorrow shalt thou eat of it all the days of thy life; thorns and thistles shall it bring forth to thee. . . ." From this taint of "Original Sin," all the rest has followed. The Fall, it is still widely believed by Christians, affected not just humanity, but the whole of creation. This is not the place for a full treatment of this account and its consequences. Most people now – excluding fundamentalists – are aware that the Genesis description, as moving and dramatic as it is, is nevertheless not historical fact. It's a mythos or spiritual story which imparts some deep, important truths. It makes the point that this is a moral universe where we must make choices. But, apart from illustrating the way in which humans use their freedom to make wrong choices with sometimes painful consequences, it is of little practical help in our understanding today. It describes the undeniable fact of evil and pain, but it throws little real light on the causes of either. That is my honest feeling anyway, and other scholars share this view.

We are not told by the Genesis story the one thing we would like to know: Why, since any God worthy of the name must have foreknown in his omniscience that humans would use their freedom badly, did he create us to be free? Why take the risk? After all, an omnipotent Creator could have arranged things differently. For example, we could have been created – through a direct fiat as Genesis tells it – always to see and choose the good and the right. A colossal amount of human and animal suffering would thus have been avoided. But, we have to think more deeply for a moment and consider where else that would have led. There may be other intelligent beings on other planets in other far-flung galaxies who are vastly our moral superiors because they don't even have an inkling of what evil is. Conceivably, their natures may permit them always and inevitably to do what is loving and good. For them, goodness would then be automatic. They would be free to choose between one good and another good alone.

But, would that be true freedom and would goodness itself truly exist when there was no alternative, no background, as it were, against which its light could be seen? The truth is that our freedom to make choices between good and evil is one of the qualities that defines us as human beings. From time immemorial we humans have treasured our freedom as a supreme value and a source of ultimate human happiness. Life on this earth would not be real, human life without this gift of inner freedom. Given a choice between being moral automatons (beings who are ethical robots), and godlike beings "knowing good and evil," most of us would not hesitate for a moment.

Others have stressed this same truth in different ways when discussing the problem of evil, but that doesn't mean it can be downplayed here. What does this freedom that we value so highly truly mean? It means supremely – if it has meaning at all – the freedom to choose evil, to reject goodness and God absolutely. Anything short of having that capacity would not be human freedom. Consequently, it should not really come as a great surprise to anyone that people do cruel and even murderous things to one another and to the rest of creation. Wars, genocides, atrocities and crimes of every kind are the "shadow side" of our moral freedom. God or the Ultimate Mind cannot give this freedom with one hand and take it away with the other, so to speak. Once risked, once inaugurated, it inexorably must have a price.

When people ask: "Why did God allow the Holocaust?" for example, my only recourse is to say I don't know. But, if humans are to be truly free, no horror, not even the calculated, methodical elimination of six million Jews by the Nazis, can be arbitrarily stopped by some act of divine intervention. We have this terrible yet eternally precious gift. It could lead us to destroy the earth itself and every living thing through an ecological or a nuclear holocaust. We really have that much choice. I am certain that God intends us to work in synergy with the powers of the entire universe. But, he has restrained his omnipotence so that we might know the joy of true freedom and attain the maturity of true "children of God." Our halting progress towards realizing the full Mind of God for humanity is intended to take place freely and willingly on our part. In his wisdom God has decided that forced obedience and automatic love are not what the cosmos needs or wants from us. (We would not want this from our own children!) We have a higher, infinitely more costly calling.

Historically, in the unending attempt to wrestle with the problem of evil, many religions and some philosophers have postulated a kind of dualism – there is a good God and an evil one. Christianity seeks to avoid a full-blown dualism by its teaching about Lucifer, the fallen angel, also known as Satan, Beelzebub or the Devil. His ultimate defeat is assured, but in the meantime he wreaks havoc. C. S. Lewis suggests that the Devil was defeated by Christ's death on the cross. The main battle has been won, in other words, he says. But alas, considerable "mopping up" still remains to be carried out. This personification of evil and the mythos of his eventual defeat are out-dated attempts to explain evil and still appeal to millions of the faithful. While powerful religious symbols, they belong to another age and place. True, they appear to take evil seriously enough, but they create more intellectual problems than they solve.

Yes, at times evil is so systemic, so gross, that it almost seems as though it has a will, mind and existence of its own – that it is a dark malignancy that attacks and warps humanity. But, ultimately, there is no "entity" or supernatural being working invisibly and plotting destruction. Given the cunning ingenuity of the human animal, coupled with the primitive drives lingering from our evolutionary past, there is explanation enough already! Each of us has what Carl Jung called "the shadow" within, and there is such a thing as a collective shadow wherever humans in groups, movements or nations are concerned. Jung pleaded for more self-knowledge on everyone's part as the way to avert the more destructive elements of the shadow. In the end, it does little good to take instead the route where our own responsibility (the other side of freedom) is neglected in favour of the excuse: "The devil made me – him, her, them – do it."

Some of the difficulties raised by the letters I excerpted above fall into better perspective when we see them in the context of the physical universe. The universe, the galaxies, and this "pale blue dot" in space, as Carl Sagan refers to our planet, are physical realities and they move or work according to observable laws. The physical universe is permeated and penetrated at every moment by the spiritual but its physicality is a raw fact. In a purely spiritual existence, children would not be accidentally killed. There would be no rape, no lynchings. There would be no empty bellies because of famine, no floods, drownings, fires or earthquakes. There would be no plagues such as the AIDS epidemic or infants born lacking a brain. But nor would there be the splendour of a waterfall, the grandeur of the thunderstorm or the majestic rolling of the sea either. Both the breathtaking beauty of the natural world as well as the most humdrum details of our ordinary lives hinge on the dependability of things. Gravity, though unseen, always works the same way. Without it, nothing as we know it would be possible. We would all fly off into space instead of remaining on the ground. But this same force can be deadly should you fall from a cliff.

This is true of all the other laws that make our universe possible in the first place. It is surely unreasonable to expect God or Ultimate Mind to sustain these laws at all times except those which are inconvenient or painful to us. This rather infantile longing to have some *deus ex machina* suspend the laws of creation solely – and "just for a moment, mind you!" – for the benefit of a specific individual or species may be perfectly natural but it doesn't stand up to scrutiny for long. Once the bullet has been fired it goes where the laws of nature determine. No hand or Hand can interfere to deflect or bring it back.

I know there are many pious people who believe that God arranges the universe and its laws – and even the weather! – every morning just for them, but that's fairly obvious nonsense. Nature has its own God-given agenda for the greater good of the whole. I agree once again with the noted ecologian, Thomas Berry, who says that, while in its "lower arc" nature may seem at times to be harsh or cruel – seen, that is, purely from our human-centred point of view – in the "larger arc" of what the cosmos is doing it is both benign and wise beyond our understanding. What appears to us as mindless destruction and devastation often leads to renewal and rebirth. It is only recently, for example, that ecologists have come to realize fully the regenerative power of forest fires caused by lightning from time to time.

In Canada each spring there is a natural phenomenon that causes many to wonder what God was up to in the act of creation. With the coming of warmer weather the northern woods are filled for a time with blackflies. They may be small but their bite is ferocious and, without proper clothing and insect repellent, they can drive you well-nigh crazy. They seem the embodiment of senseless malice, a scourge on the earth. Yet, according to biologists, these pests (from our point of view) are essential to the overall ecology of the woods, streams and lakes whose beauty we so enjoy. Blackflies help pollinate blueberries, keep – through their larvae – the fish population healthy, and provide food for migratory waterfowl, for dragonflies and for many of the loveliest songbirds in the forest.

Earthquakes, floods, tornadoes and other such "acts of God" are not divine punishments for human sins – although it's true that the religiously superstitious response has often been to interpret them that way. They're part of the very majesty of the natural world which so powerfully evokes our joy, wonder and awe. When we build our cities on known fault lines in the crust of the earth (as in California), on flood plains or low-lying coastal lands (as in Bangladesh) it makes little sense to complain about divine injustice when disasters strike. Our habitual hubris and indifference to our environment (much of the worst flooding in Asia, for example, is the result of cutting down the forests on nearby mountainsides) often cause or greatly compound any tragedy.

On the matter of pain itself, whether physical, mental or emotional, we need to consider whether it has any positive side. What is its role in the evolutionary story of life? Without question, were it not for the phenomenon of pain we would not be here in our present form at all. Pain tells us both that we are alive and that some aspect of our well-being and even possibly our survival is threatened. Inability to feel pain – as with leprosy, for example, or any disease causing severe neuropathy – leads to injury, loss of one's extremities, and, ultimately, to death. Pain is nature's warning signal. It is essential to healing and health. Without it, the cosmos could never have finally brought forth self-reflective consciousness, the summit of creation.

One day someone will write a book on pain in which its role in the advancement both of biological life and of human culture and civilization will be investigated and told. It has been one of the key factors making possible the whole unfolding of evolution. The aphorism "no pain, no gain" is certainly true of the story of our species. As Aeschylus once said long ago in his play *Agamemnon*, "He who learns must suffer," meaning that it is the lot of human beings to learn through suffering. Some of the greatest artistic, literary and musical achievements of our race have been produced by or accompanied by great suffering and endurance. There is also great truth in C. S. Lewis's view that suffering can break through our human indolence and pride and bring us closer to God. "Pain plants the flag of truth in the fortress of the rebel soul," he writes. However, I personally hold no brief for the idea that God deliberately sends a particular illness, loss or other grief to teach us a lesson, test us, or improve us in some way. Yet, the pain can be seen *after the fact* to have had positive effects. It can lead to insights and maturity – a spiritual step ahead – we never expected. We can learn things through it we never knew before, about life, about ourselves, about our relationships to others, and about God. Certainly there is such a thing as senseless, needless pain, as, for example, when medical technology unduly prolongs the dying of the terminally ill. But, most pain, particularly the worst kind of all, that of the mind in grief, depression, or remorse, ultimately can be redeemed. Like Jacob of old in his struggle with the angel, we can wrestle with it and extract a blessing. Jacob's suffering was very real. He always limped thereafter. But, he was a changed man as a result of his experience and very much for the better as the story goes.

Now a word about animal suffering. It is of primary importance to me when thinking about this to recognize and admit from the outset that the greatest and most extensive suffering of animals is produced by human ignorance, folly, cruelty, thoughtlessness and greed. There are few greater blots on the history of humanity than our treatment of animals. We are bound up together in the amazing "bundle of life" with them and share their characteristics as well as their fate to a degree many still don't realize. There is no surer test of the morality of a nation or people than how it relates to other species. Through senseless slaughter, through "sport" hunting, through destruction of habitats, and through needless experimentation for military or cosmetic purposes we have increased the pain of innocent animals a thousandfold. I have written extensively in my book *God Help Us* and in many columns over the years about the needless cruelty of slaughterhouses and of the reasons for vegetarianism or something as close to it as practically possible. I loathe hunting, except in the case of those who need to do it for their food supply, for example, some Aboriginal peoples.

Having got that out of the way, of course, a problem still remains. I frankly do not know why God created a world in which nature is often "red in tooth and claw." I say "often" because those who advance this objection to the idea of a loving God are guilty at times of vastly overstating their case. Large numbers of species, including some of the largest mammals of all, do not kill prey. We are learning more today as well of how much love and caring and of how much peaceful co-operation exists between various animal species, not to mention between bacteria and animals. Yet violence in the animal kingdom cannot be denied. We have all winced or turned away from our television sets while watching a documentary that explicitly shows the slow and seemingly torturous deaths endured by many living things as they are caught and eaten by others.

This reality must not be evaded or whitewashed. Surely, we think, it could have been otherwise. In my own attempts to understand this mystery, I've found two factors of some help to me. One is that God seems to have provided a built-in mercy of a kind. Many insects and other life forms first stun or neutralize the nervous system of their victims before devouring them. This is true of some species of insects, reptiles and fish, for example. We project our feelings onto the hapless quarry, but in reality, apart from the initial fear, there is little or no pain involved. There is evidence as well that when the larger carnivores first seize their prey the animal is flooded by the kind of endorphins or other natural narcotics also produced by the human brain *in extremis*. The noted missionary, Dr. David Livingstone, in a well-known passage in his diaries, describes an encounter he once had with a man-eating lion. Once it had seized him in its jaws, he relates, his whole being was gripped by an amazing sense of calm, even approaching euphoria.

The second insight is equally important to me. That is, without the hunter and the pursued some of the greatest and most beautiful aspects of the natural world would never have developed. We all marvel at the speed of the cheetah and at its awesome hunting skills. We are deeply moved as well by the gracefulness in flight of the gazelle or wildebeest. But they belong together. In fact, they have in an evolutionary way produced each other. The same is true of the eagle and the hawk, whose stunning diving abilities have evolved in tandem with hares' and rabbits' long legs and skill in evading pursuit, or the intriguing, equally amazing defensive tactics and markings of songbirds. We could not have the majesty and sleek, though sinister, glories of sharks and other predatory fish without the kaleidoscopic colourings and manoeuvrings of tropical and other fish. While seemingly cruel in some of its aspects, the phenomenon of evolution could not have taken place without this close interdependence of hunter and hunted. In the final analysis, the pain which nature so abundantly reveals has also its redemptive or positive side. It seems redemption is impossible without pain, given the cosmic evolution that ultimately produced ourselves. In humans, the entire universe comes not just to consciousness but to self-aware consciousness. In us, nature can ponder itself and ask the kind of questions we are asking here. That, as physicist Paul Davies says, is a consequence of unparalleled significance.

Finally, the believer has one contribution to this discussion that the unbeliever can never have. What ultimately helps me most with the problem of pain is my belief that God shares in our deepest suffering and inspires us to put an end to unnecessary suffering whether human or non-human to the degree that it is possible. The entire witness, for example, of the Judeo-Christian tradition is that in love and mercy God is with us in our darkest hour. That is the deepest meaning of the Christian mythos or story of redemption. I am not much helped by many orthodox dogmas about the Cross and the Death and Resurrection of Jesus Christ. But this is holy ground all the same because at its deepest levels of meaning it conveys the truth that we are never alone in our anxieties, griefs, and pains. Nor are other animals either. God "sees the sparrow fall." The Christian "good news" is really not about being "saved" through this belief or that commitment. It's that God does not stand aloof from our troubles. He knows our deepest woes and has promised that when we pass through the "shadow of the valley of death" even there he is with us. There is resurrection on the other side of every tragedy for those who put their ultimate trust in him.

Now, even after all of this I am deeply aware of having just scraped the surface and of perhaps raising as many questions as I tried to answer. To do a complete job one would have to know the Mind of God as only God himself can do. In the end, as at the beginning, there is a great mystery. I can only say that I feel and see evidence on every side that, pain or no pain, evil or no evil, the power and source behind the universe is the loving God so movingly spoken about and trusted in by Christ and by so many millions of believers, Christians and non-Christians alike, through the ages and still today.

It is possible to be highly sensitive to the injustices and sufferings of life and hold this faith. For example, Jesus, one of the most clear-headed realists of all time, had no illusions about the pain and suffering around him. Yet, the record makes it abundantly plain that he believed in a providential universe at the same time. Incidentally, while nobody has a corner on goodness or on the fight to make this a better life for all, the ones who have most impressed me, especially in my travels in poorer parts of the world, for doing something about pain and evil rather than just complaining about them, are those whose radical commitment is born of their spiritual beliefs. It was true in former times. It remains so today.

One final thought. Religious belief in an afterlife in which we will be made whole and grow into or fulfil our true spiritual nature in the presence of God undoubtedly owes much of its power to our deeply felt need to have everything make sense one day. It's the final recourse in our thirst for seeing justice done, the ultimate answer to the question of why God causes suffering posed by Job in the Hebrew Bible, and to the problem of theodicy. If death were the end of everything, if it were without hope, then God would indeed be some kind of capricious, sadistic monster. If, on the other hand, death is but a transition stage or a door to a new and wider dimension of consciousness, then, as Socrates pointed out just before he took the fatal cup, it is not something to be feared but to be accepted joyfully. "If death be of such a nature, I say that to die is to gain," he says in Plato's *Apology*.

Since, as I noted earlier, I have already set out at length in my book *Life After Death* both my research and my reasons for believing in it, I will not cover the same ground again here. Like Carl Jung more recently and like St. Paul long ago, I'm wholly persuaded that the human imagination is quite incapable of conceiving the full glory of the next phase of human existence. And, as I also made clear in *Life After Death*, I believe the animal world – all sentient beings – is included in God's plans for our eternity as well. As the Book of Revelation says, there will be new heavens and a new earth. Our present experience of pain and evil, then, is for a very limited time only. Its full meaning and its total healing will one day be seen in the perspective of the eternal. To borrow from the poet Robert Frost, that will make "all the difference."

5

Cosmic Consciousness

As we have already seen, there is more talk and there are more best-selling books today about spirituality (the "S word" as it is now sometimes referred to) than at any time in recent memory. Something is definitely stirring in the human soul as we approach the year 2000 A.D. Naturally, there are lots of "junk food" or quick-fix approaches being offered. But overall a widespread, serious search is afoot, and for the most part it's taking place outside traditional religious institutions. The reader at this point has the right to ask: What is spirituality anyway and what would a spirituality for a new millennium be like? I will answer as best I can.

Essentially, spirituality is about the inner life or spirit of each of us as it relates to the unseen world of Spirit or of God. It's the name we give to the dimension of seeing and living that goes far beyond the material world to deeper truths and eternal values. To be a spiritual person means realizing one's true nature as an expression of the "true Light which gives light to every person who comes into the world," to quote John's Gospel. It includes the profound faith and trust that there is a meaning and purpose to life, that we are destined one day to experience another plane of existence. The challenge, I believe, as we consider a faith for 2001 and beyond, is to find a basis and form for a spirituality that moves beyond anything our species as a whole has ever before thought of or practised. With this in mind, consider the following:

The story in the *Globe and Mail* rated three inches in a column headed: "Briefly." Given the horror of what it described, its almost throwaway "play" in the paper was a stark symbol of how far we have gone as a species in our tolerance of the unspeakable. An international aid agency had issued a report saying wars have killed over 1.5 million children since 1984 and injured 4 million. It said that in the decade from 1984 to 1994 at the hands of soldiers millions of children have been raped, have seen their parents butchered, and have been forced to become soldiers themselves. "More than 4 million children have been disabled, maimed, blinded and brain-damaged. More than 12 million have lost their homes," Save the Children reported.

I am not citing this news to depress you. This chapter is about hope for the way ahead. But we have to face some terrible truths. One could list a hundred of them, but these grim facts about children suffice to make the point that we human beings must change radically if war and atrocities are ever to cease. But how – given our addiction to violence against our fellows and against other life forms – can such a key transformation come about? We could go on to ask the same question with regard to our planetary crisis over the devastation of the environment or over global poverty. I have mentioned before the ecologian, Fr. Thomas Berry, author of *The Dream of the Earth* and other books. He says humanity must "reinvent itself" in order to relate differently to the earth. Yes, but, supposing it were possible, that still deals only with the environmental problem. To eliminate war and the savagery of humans to one another requires something more, I believe. The same could be said about solving the conundrum of how to find enough satisfactory work for people all over the world while at the same time trying to replace the current model of unbridled growth and economic expansion. Development alone only further threatens our already sadly degraded biosphere. There is talk of "sustainable" development as the new paradigm, but so far it exists more in theory than actuality. Given the enormous problems facing us, we need a new paradigm and a wholly new approach.

A partial clue can be discerned in Albert Einstein's words about the way each of us is an integral part of a whole, the universe, yet we experience ourselves, our thoughts and feelings, as separate from all the rest. This amounts to a kind of optical delusion of consciousness, he said: "The delusion is a prison for us, restricting us to our personal desires and to affection for a few persons nearest to us. Our task must be to free ourselves . . . by widening our circle of compassion to embrace all living creatures and the whole of nature in its beauty." Einstein went on to note that nobody can fully achieve this but that the striving for such a goal is, in itself, a part of the liberation needed and "a foundation for inner security."

Before Einstein made these comments, in 1901 a remarkable book by a Canadian doctor, Richard Maurice Bucke, went even further in pointing the way to the kind of "conversion" or quantum leap we need to make if we are to survive, solve our many dilemmas and become truly human. The book, still in print, is *Cosmic Consciousness*. Bucke (1837-1902) had an extraordinary career. He was born of "good middle class English stock," as he put it, and grew up with little formal education (though he had access to his father's extensive library and read avidly) on a backwoods Canadian farm not far from London, Ontario. He was always deeply concerned about spirituality. But, as he tells us in his book (in which he refers to himself in the third person), even as a child he didn't accept all the doctrines of the Christian Church "but as soon as old enough to dwell at all on such themes conceived that Jesus was a man – great and good no doubt, but a man." He was also convinced at an early age "that no one would ever be condemned to everlasting pain." Bucke's mother died when he was only a few years old and he became estranged from his father while in his early teens. Consequently, at age sixteen, he left home "to live or die as might happen." For five years he wandered over North America, working on farms, on railways, on steamboats and in the placer mine diggings of western Nevada. Once, while crossing the mountains on foot in late fall, going from Lake Tahoe to Sacramento, he almost starved and froze to death. He lost one foot and most of the other subsequently because of the severe frostbite. Bucke came back to Canada at the age of twenty-one and with a modest inheritance from his dead mother enrolled in medical school at McGill University. He graduated with high honours four years later.

Outside of his medical studies, he was reading broadly, including Charles Darwin's *Origin of Species* and "much poetry, especially such as seemed to him free and fearless." He learned French to read Auguste Comte, Hugo and Renan, and German that he might read Goethe, particularly *Faust*. Then, at the age of thirty, he came upon Walt Whitman's *Leaves of Grass*. Instinctively, he felt that there was something in Whitman that resonated with his own deep spiritual hunger. He read the *Leaves* "passionately" but "for several years derived little from them." Finally, he says, light broke in and some of it at least began to make marvellous sense. He was later to develop a close friendship with the great American poet. He hosted Whitman on a several-week visit to Canada, including a cruise on the Saguenay River, Quebec – a visit portrayed in the film *Beautiful Dreamers*, starring Colm Feore and Rip Torn – and eventually Whitman made him one of his three literary executors. A psychiatrist and an eager scholar, Bucke went on to become superintendent of what was then known as the London Insane Asylum for twenty-five years and quickly became internationally known for his advanced ideas on mental and nervous disorders. However, the pivotal point in his life came one spring night when he was thirty-six.

Bucke was in London, England, and had spent the evening with friends reading poetry, especially Whitman. He left at midnight and had a long drive in a horse-drawn cab ahead. In his account of what happened, he was in "a state of quiet, almost passive enjoyment," his mind under the influence of the images, emotions and ideas he had just shared. Quite suddenly, without warning of any kind, he found himself wrapped around by what seemed like "a flame coloured cloud." His first thought was that London was on fire. The next moment he realized that the light was within himself.

At once, there came upon him a "sense of exultation, of immense joyousness accompanied . . . by an intellectual illumination quite impossible to describe." Into his brain "streamed one momentary lightning-flash of Brahmic [divine] Splendour which has ever since enlightened his life. Upon his heart fell one drop of Brahmic bliss, leaving thenceforward for always an after taste of heaven." With bliss came knowledge. He says he did not come to believe but actually "saw and knew" that the cosmos "is not dead matter but a living presence, that the soul of man is immortal, that the universe is so built and ordered that . . . all things work together for the good of each, that the foundation principle of the world is what we call love and that the happiness of every one is in the long run absolutely certain." He saw much more as well. He wrote that he learned more within the few seconds during which the illumination lasted than in previous months or even years of study, and that he learned much "that no study could ever have taught."

This enlightenment wholly changed him. He felt his spiritual eyes had been opened, that he had been "born again." In *Cosmic Consciousness*, he gives the results of years spent digesting this experience and studying all those who, like Buddha, Moses, Jesus, Paul, Muhammad – and lesser lights such as Dante, Blake and Whitman – had in his opinion a more intense and lasting awareness or consciousness. This, he was convinced, was the "Christ mind" or saving vision needed on humanity's road ahead. Bucke believed that cosmic consciousness, this sense of the deep unity of all parts of the universe and of the amazing love binding it all together, is the next step in the development of humans. What the forerunners and mystics of all faiths have known, every person must eventually come to know. Just as we each have ordinary consciousness which we share with other animals and self-aware consciousness which makes us unique (at least in our corner of the galaxy), one day all humans will have cosmic consciousness as their birthright, he argued. All the great modern religions, Bucke contended, have their origins with individuals who had this kind of awareness, "beginning with Taoism and Buddhism." From their lives and thinking, much of the literature and civilization of the whole world has flowed over the past three thousand years.

While cosmic consciousness has as its primary characteristic a deep sense of the life and order of the universe, other elements in it include "an intellectual enlightenment or illumination which alone would place the individual on a new plane of existence – would make him almost a member of a new species. To this is added a state of moral exaltation, an indescribable feeling of elevation, elation and joyousness, and a quickening of the moral sense, which is fully as striking and more important both to the individual and to the race than is the enhanced intellectual power. With these come . . . a sense of immortality, a consciousness of eternal life, not a conviction that he shall have this, but the consciousness that he has it already."

Bucke was quick to realize that the experience he had tasted so briefly had been written about many times before. He found it in the biblical descriptions of the life of St. Paul who, in addition to many other mystical experiences, tells us that he was once caught up into "the seventh heaven" and told secrets too sacred to utter. He found it in Eastern religions, in some truly great poetry, and in the writings of mystics of all faiths down the ages. What was different about Bucke's approach was that for the first time here was an expert in the science of his day using scientific theories, methods and language to express the nature and meaning of the ultimate in spiritual experience. For him, this sense of "union with God" or with the totality of things and of seeing the deeper patterns of oneness behind the apparent diversities of life was, above all, the next evolutionary step for humanity. He believed, rightly, that only this vital awareness of our profound unity with *all* other humans, the rest of the cosmos and the Ultimate Love beneath it can save us from destroying everything.

It's significant that although Bucke was deeply spiritual and had a lovely chapel (still in use today) built on the grounds of the London hospital for the use of his patients as part of the healing process, he continued to find traditional Christianity too limited by its own dogmas. In the end, it was Walt Whitman and the witness to cosmic consciousness in *Leaves of Grass* that became his own guiding light. This is not the place for a full account of Whitman's philosophy, but it's clear from his writing that his creativity and his strongly spiritual outlook on life were inextricably bound up together. Consider these lovely lines from *Leaves of Grass*:

> And I know that the hand of God is the
>   elderhand of my own,
> And I know that the spirit of God is the elder
>   brother of my own,
> And that all the men ever born are also my
>   brothers. . . . and the women my sisters
>   and lovers,
> And that a kelson of the creation is love.

When I first read this passage, I had never come across the word kelson before. The Concise Oxford Dictionary said that it derives from the word keel – as of a boat – and an unexplained suffix, son. The reference, then, is to the line of timber used to fasten the floor-timbers at the bottom of a ship to its keel. In Whitman's imagery, the meaning is then clear. He is summing up his vision that he is one with God and with all humanity from the beginning of time with the resounding statement of faith that the very bond or foundation keel of all creation is love. This is an amazing credo for one who belonged to no church and scandalized many of the pious by his enthusiastic affirmation of the body and the senses. Experts on Whitman and his work, however, know that this credo is a grounding theme of his poetry. His passionate grasp of life itself stemmed from an ongoing, mystical insight into the nature of things – a clear example, in Bucke's thinking particularly, of cosmic consciousness. I would just add that Whitman did not believe in the ultimate goodness and benevolence of God and in life after death because of some Pollyanna-type wishful thinking or ethereal dreaming. What strikes you as you read him and struggle with the various levels of meaning is that Whitman knew life intimately in all its rawness. For many months, during the slaughter of the American Civil War, he nursed the wounded and dying. He saw the torn, lacerated bodies and the agonies of minds and emotions stretched beyond all endurance. He knew that life can be hell and that hate and injustice often seem to be in control. Yet he also knew that the "kelson" of the universe is divine love.

It was Bucke's conviction that just as self-aware consciousness had slowly evolved, with at first only a few individuals here and there possessing it fully, so it would happen with this next stage, cosmic consciousness. For the past several millennia, its appearance has been sporadic, yet leading to the founding of the great religions. But, over the last five hundred years the process, he believed, had begun to quicken. He wrote of himself: "The view he takes is that our descendants will sooner or later reach, as a race, the condition of cosmic consciousness, just as, long ago, our ancestors passed from simple consciousness to self-consciousness. He believes that this step in evolution is even now being made since it is clear to him both that men with the faculty in question are becoming more and more common and also that as a race we are approaching nearer and nearer to that stage of the self-conscious mind from which the transition to the cosmic consciousness is effected."

Had Bucke been alive and written his book today, it could not seem more modern, more in synchrony with the leading edge of both research into consciousness and new religious thinking. The fact that it was written a century ago makes it a prophetic work.

Before leaving him, let's hear what he had to say about the future of religion once the entire race possesses cosmic consciousness. He wrote that "all religions known and named today will be melted down. The human soul will be revolutionized." Does this mean that religion itself will vanish? Quite the contrary. "Religion will absolutely dominate the race. It will not depend on tradition. It will not be believed and disbelieved. It will not be a part of life, belonging to certain hours, times, occasions. It will not be in sacred books nor in the mouths of priests. It will not dwell in churches and meetings and forms and days. . . . It will not teach a future immortality nor future glories, for immortality and glory will live in every heart as sight in every eye. Doubt of God and of eternal life will be as impossible as is now doubt of existence; the evidence of each will be the same. Religion will govern every minute of every day of all of life." He goes on to say that no clergy or other intermediaries will be necessary since there will be direct, unmistakable intercourse with the Creator. "Each soul will feel and know itself to be immortal, will feel and know that the entire universe with all its good and with all its beauty is for it and belongs to it forever." This new age will be as far removed from the world of today as this is from the world our race knew before the arrival of full self-aware consciousness aeons ago. If you replace his word "religion" with "spirituality," you have, I believe, an accurate description of what a truly spiritual humanity would experience.

I was astonished not long ago, after writing a newspaper column about Bucke's book and our need for a new kind of consciousness, to receive a number of letters from people who described mystical experiences very similar to his. For example, one young married woman, who holds a responsible job as a scientist working for the Canadian government, described how, on the night of her thirty-fifth birthday, she had a mystical dream. In it, she says, "I was light. I was in the light, I was outside the light, I was flowing as the light. In those moments, I felt unified with God and connected with all humanity and the earth itself." At the same time, she was given the knowledge that she was meant to "help uncover the role of spirituality in the workplace." Today she spends much of her time giving lectures on "Spirituality in the Workplace and Its Relationship to Sustainable Development" to senior managers both in government and in private business in Canada and the United States.

Considering the number of accounts of near-death experiences – over eight million North Americans have had an NDE, and many millions more have now been reported from around the world – and the fact that researchers in both Britain and the United States report that close to half the population have had some type of mystical experience of being in the presence of the Light and of knowing the unity of all things, it is evident that Bucke's predictions are, to some extent at least, coming true. People who have had such encounters are deeply and permanently changed by them. They do not for the most part find themselves going back to church, synagogue or temple. But, with almost one voice they do say that they have become more spiritual, more truly moral, more aware of the kind of love and the kind of unities at the foundation of the universe of which Bucke, Whitman and others have written so eloquently.

You don't have to accept every argument or detail in a work like Bucke's *Cosmic Consciousness* to realize the truth of its main thrust. Moreover, you don't have to forswear all formal religion to experience the kind of spirituality I'm writing about in this book. You don't even have to have some seemingly supernatural intervention or mystical encounter as Bucke did on that memorable night in the hansom cab. But, if our spirituality does not embrace every person on the face of the earth, if it does not also embrace other living things and the whole of the cosmos, if it depends on somebody else or on something else (a sacred book, place or rite), and finally, if it is not experienced as real by oneself, then it is not a spirituality for now or for the future.

I am open to the possibility of having a mystical experience, some "flight of the alone to the Alone," as Plotinus described it, but I have not had one to date and, like many of you, may well never do so. You can be open to it but you cannot command it. At the same time, however, I believe Einstein was right. You don't have to have the experience of ultimate union with the universe to escape the "delusion" of separation and to begin to widen your circle of compassion to embrace all living things and nature itself. As he rightly said, being aware and then striving to achieve the basic elements of a cosmic consciousness is "part of the liberation" needed at this time. Until we achieve full cosmic consciousness we can act as though we had done so. The only religious outlook or spirituality that makes sense now is one that is not just global but cosmic in its scope. All those faith-stances that are focused solely on human beings and their needs or caught up in denominational or other rivalries – that maintain that unless you are one of us, part of this faith or that experience, you're outside the fold and "lost" – are too stilted and parochial in their present mind-set to lead the way forward. An English vicar, J. B. Phillips, once wrote a popular book, *Your God Is Too Small*. The problem with the major religions today is not just that their vision of God is still too small; in too many cases, their understanding of the kind of faith and spirituality appropriate to the twenty-first century is by far too small as well. The day of divisive and narrowly fixated religions is passing away. Only those which adopt an inclusive cosmic understanding will survive.

This does not mean we are moving to a kind of syncretism – a meshing together of highlights from all the various religions into some kind of super-faith or super-church. A global religious porridge in the name of ecumenism is neither necessary nor desirable. Each faith at its best has its own contribution, its own unique ethos, to add to the overall human vision of God. But, a true cosmic consciousness will enable humanity for the first time to transcend former isolations and dogmatisms and see fully for the first time that there is a profound unity underlying and vastly exceeding all the more obvious surface differences. The urge to convert others to one's own particular faith or to scorn all those who differ will vanish in the knowledge that there is a far greater wisdom, an infinitely larger horizon, in the light of which all previous certainties will seem partial and pale.

A final note. The day after I finished writing the above, I read a newspaper story headed "Futurist hails birth of a global brain." Robert Muller, a futurist who is currently chancellor of the United Nations' University for Peace in Costa Rica and who was assistant secretary-general to the U.N. from 1970 to 1986, told a reporter in an interview that out of the chaos of the twentieth century a "planetary consciousness" is emerging. As we head toward the year 2000, Muller said, we have a global brain for the first time in human history. People are linked as never before by computer technology and knowledge is exploding. The idea that a communications-based global brain is part of an evolutionary leap by humans is, of course, not new. The French priest-scientist Pierre Teilhard de Chardin earlier this century concluded that humans were headed towards a unification of the species into a single thinking whole. He chose the word noosphere (from the Greek word, *nous*, meaning mind) to refer to the overall effect of human minds on the planet, a planetary consciousness. A classic work on this same subject is Peter Russell's 1982 book, *The Global Brain*. But, the story about Muller underlined again for me that the transformation to cosmic consciousness is not a matter just of mysticism or some unknown evolutionary process alone. The technological creation of an electronic "nervous system" or global brain embracing every nook and corner of the globe and the immediacy of contact it allows between us and our fellow humans everywhere have laid the groundwork for the universal cosmic consciousness still to be fully realized one day.

6

A Fuzzy Faith

My wife and I wandered into a trading post-type store in the Temagami region of Ontario on a recent trip. Some wiseacre wall plaques immediately caught my eye. I got a few strange glances as I chuckled out loud at one of them. The title was, "Why Worry?" Here is roughly how it went:

> There are only two things to worry about.
> Either you are sick or you are well.
> If you are well, there's nothing to worry about.
> If you are sick, there are only two things to worry about.
> Either you will get well or you will die.
> If you get well, there's nothing to worry about.
> If you die, there are only two things to worry about.
> Either you will go to heaven or to hell.
> If you go to heaven, there's nothing to worry about.

If you go to hell, you'll be so damned busy shaking
    hands with all your friends you won't have
    time to worry!

There is a serious point behind this humorous bit
of folk "wisdom." It illustrates the folly inherent in
the most common, most dangerous oversimpli-
fication known to human thought: the either-or
syndrome. Few things are more seductive than the
temptation to see life and its challenges as a series of
"either-or" propositions. But no approach to others,
to our fundamental human relationships, or to religious and moral questions has had more potential
for harm. It appears superficially to be logical.
Indeed, as we shall see, it has been the prevailing
approach in Western culture ever since Aristotle
defined logic for us. It has left an indelible imprint
upon orthodox traditions of Christianity. Most
modern science still lives by its black-and-white
approach. Yet, in its failure to recognize the deep
complexities of the real world, the ambiguities and
"greyness" of actual thought and experience, it leads
to error, harsh judgementalism and bitter divisions.
Both in the past and in the present it has led to both
political and religious violence.

Aristotle's legacy to Western religious thought
and to modern science has been the logic that something cannot at the same time be one thing and not
be it. White or black. It is either one or the other.
Both science and orthodox Christianity have taken

the position that all things are either absolutely true or absolutely false. There is truth and there is heresy. There are facts and there are non-facts. Jesus was either God or he was not. The sky is either blue or not blue. This approach has simplified things enormously for both traditions. The great problem, however, with this kind of logic – apart from the divisions and bitterness it has caused and the way science tends to say "either our way or no knowledge at all" – is that it results in an enormous distortion. As the American professor Bart Kosko has put it, all facts are a matter of degree. They are always fuzzy or vague or inexact to some degree, and it is a fallacy for science to treat the grey or fuzzy facts of the universe as if they were the black-and-white facts of mathematics. You can, of course, be precise in math, you can use the either-or logic to your heart's content because math is not the real world. It's a construct of rules and symbols. Albert Einstein himself made this important distinction in his book *Geometry and Experience*: "So far as the laws of mathematics refer to reality, they are not certain. And so far as they are certain, they do not refer to reality."

Kosko, whose 1993 book, *Fuzzy Thinking: The New Science of Fuzzy Logic*, is one of the most helpful works I have read in a long time, is on the faculty of the University of Southern California and holds degrees in philosophy, economics, mathematics and electrical engineering. But, most importantly, he is the leading proponent and popularizer of an entirely new scientific movement based upon what is called fuzzy logic. His best-selling textbook on the subject, *Neural Networks and Fuzzy Systems*, is difficult for the layman – too many equations. But in *Fuzzy Thinking* he has opened, at least for me, a new way of understanding religion and spirituality. Here are the opening sentences of his preface: "One day I learned that science was not true. . . . The God of the twentieth century was no longer God. There was a mistake and everyone in science seemed to make it. They said all things were true or false." While no one has ever produced a single fact about the world that is 100 per cent true or 100 per cent false, scientists continue to speak and act as if they had, he contends.

Kosko goes on to show how Eastern belief systems from Lao-tze's Taoism to modern Zen Buddhism in Japan follow a very different path from the one laid down by Aristotle. For the Buddha, "the first step in his belief system was to break through the black-and-white world of words, pierce the bivalent [either-or] veil and see the world as it is, see it filled with 'contradictions,' with things and not-things, with roses that are both red and not-red, with A and not-A." This kind of logic is "fuzzy." Instead of either-or, it's a matter of both-and, of several possibilities at the same time, of "greyness." Surprisingly, the more you apply this approach to the natural world, to moral questions, and to religious truths, the more accurate and insightful it appears.

Life is not black and white. Nor is it static and

fixed. As Heraclitus said long ago, everything is flowing into something else. It is hard to say where a finger ends and the hand begins, or to detail precisely where foothills become mountains, when the day really closes and night begins, or when night is over and the day has started. Everywhere in science, from Werner Heisenberg's Uncertainty Principle (which states that you can never accurately measure both the speed and the position of subatomic particles at the same time because to do one interferes with the other) to the drawing of the most detailed maps imaginable, we are in reality faced with fuzziness, imprecision, both-and. A law of science is not really a law like two plus two equals four. As Kosko points out, "Laws of science state tendencies we have recently observed in our corner of the universe. The best you can say about them is so far, so good. . . . Their truth is a matter of degree and is always up for grabs." True science is always tentative, open to revision and change.

In case all of this seems rather ethereal or impractical, it's worth knowing that fuzzy logic or thinking is now at the very cutting edge of the newest technology. Because it mimics more closely the way our own minds really work, it is today being used in a vast range of machines so they will "think" more like human beings. For example, Japanese and Korean companies are already applying fuzzy technology to the tune of billions of dollars a year for such products as air-conditioners (instead of giving a blast of cold

air or nothing at all, "fuzzy" air-conditioners constantly measure the precise room temperature and
emit a corresponding degree of cool air); computers;
cameras and camcorders; automobile engines, brakes,
transmissions, and cruise controls; dishwashers; ele-
vators; washing machines and dryers; microwave
ovens and televisions. Fuzzy logic is used in making
palm-sized computers that can recognize and trans-
late handwritten characters. Soon there will be
"smart" artificial body parts and much more. Fuzzy
logic can even be applied to ethical questions such as,
when does life begin? Is it at the moment of concep-
tion? When the foetus is three months or six months
old? At the time of birth? Fuzzy logic escapes the
either-or by saying that life begins at all these times –
to a degree.

You may still be wondering, however, what any of
this has to do with faith and spirituality. The answer
is, everything. The major reason for orthodox
Christianity's distortion of the original message of
Jesus, for example, lies in the imposition on it,
through Aristotle and later the great Aristotelian
scholar St. Thomas Aquinas, of a Western, either-or
logic completely foreign to it. The entire edifice of
Christian dogma is based upon a true-or-false mentality and outlook. But, in the process, the origins of the
faith have been forgotten. Contradictions, tensions,
ambiguities and multivalence (manifold options)
abound in the New Testament, particularly in the

recorded teachings of Jesus. These are traditionally ignored, explained away or simply forced to fit our Western preference for the simplest view, that of bivalence, of either this or that. The most classic example, and one which always intrigued me until I solved it – at least to my own satisfaction – with fuzzy logic, is one you will never hear fundamentalist preachers talk about. They like a black-and-white approach. It fits their need for simplicity. Thus, they are quite fond of the saying of Jesus in Matthew 12:30: "He that is not with me is against me; and he that gathereth not with me scattereth abroad." By itself it seems more like the thinking of Aristotle than of the Buddha. But these same clergy completely avoid the following text from the earliest Gospel, Mark 9:40: "For he that is not against us is on our part." Our instinct is to say, well, which is it to be? One or the other must be right. (Incidentally, the very difficulty of this Markan verse virtually guarantees its authenticity. The rule of thumb is that the more difficult a text is to understand, the less likely it is to have been invented by some editor at a later date. Changes to any ancient text are always aimed at clarification, not the reverse.) The full reality is that both statements are true and must be held and understood together. Together they make for a faith marked more by inclusion than by exclusion. Only those few who are consciously and vigorously acting in opposition are to be considered as outside the movement. I believe that this kind of both-and logic is the only way to grasp what Jesus was trying to communicate.

Once you see Jesus not as a Western philosopher but as a teacher in the tradition of Judaism and of Eastern-style thinking, a wholly fresh light is shed upon the parables and short, pithy sayings of the Synoptic Gospels. Contradictions and obviously exaggerated remarks – for example, if thine eye offend thee, pluck it out – can be seen in a totally different light. At one moment he talks of coming to bring peace. At another, he says he has not come to bring peace but a sword. We are to love one another as ourselves and yet if a person doesn't "hate" his "father, and mother, and wife, and children, and brethren, and sisters, yea and his own life also," he cannot be a disciple (Luke 14:26). The Kingdom of God is spoken of as "having come," as "being present now" and as "coming in the future." Its reality belongs to all three tenses, past, present and future. Nothing could be more different from either-or. Because his concern was with real life and with real human beings, neither of which adhere to simple, black-and-white categories, Jesus' teaching was of necessity fuzzy in Kosko's technical sense of the word.

One could, of course, also apply fuzzy logic to St. Paul. He writes of being both weak and strong at one and the same time. Salvation is by faith and grace alone, not by "works," and yet he insists at the same time that we have to work at it because one day "each man's work will be made manifest." He tells the Christians at Philippi to "work out your own salvation. . . . " Paul holds together the contradictions of a total assurance on the one hand – "I know whom I have believed and am persuaded" – and a quite tentative agnosticism on the other – "Now we know in part, and we prophesy in part," and "For now we see through a glass darkly; but then face to face: now I know in part; but then I shall know as even also I am known."

There are profound implications for our own spirituality in all of this as we face the future. Belief in and commitment to the Mind and Presence we call God is no longer a matter of dividing society and the world into "them and us," into those who hold "the truth" and those who are in error, into true believers and non-believers. We are all believers to a degree. We are all unbelievers, even the most devout – to a degree. The man in the Gospels whom I cited earlier and who prayed, "Lord, I believe. Help thou my unbelief!" was a fuzzy believer. Despite their denials, even agnostics live by faith (atheists certainly do). It is all a matter of degree. This brings a new tolerance to the spiritual scene and a new flexibility – and hence creativity – to contemporary moral dilemmas, from abortion to euthanasia. This doesn't mean that in the spiritual life we will never be sure of anything, always searching and never finding; it does mean a fresh openness, less dogmatism, and an ability to live with the reality of paradoxes and contradictions rather than the perpetual fantasy of believing it has to be either one thing or the other.

It would help enormously in human spiritual progress at this critical juncture if the Christian Church and Christians in general could adopt a "fuzzier" understanding of their own tenets and of other faiths. Hold all the various core doctrines by all means if they must, but in a much more open, less dogmatic way. The fundamentalist and conservative branches, which seem to be enjoying a resurgence of a kind, particularly need to take this approach. But the more liberal churches need consciousness-raising here as well. I have already described my somewhat elastic and at times uncomfortable relationship with my own Anglican denomination. My wife and I try to support our local parish. There's an active, growing congregation and an able, popular rector. But we are finding it increasingly difficult to get much out of the services. In spite of a determination to rise above or ignore the more literal and either-or aspects of the worship, as well as the parochial idea of who really belongs to the chosen of the Lord, more often than not we come away feeling less spiritually charged than before we attended.

On one Trinity Sunday, for example, the rector wisely decided to let his female assistant curate give the homily on the difficult topic of the doctrine of the Holy Trinity. (Trinity Sunday is often the time when a guest preacher is invited!) She began by stating categorically, in the best either-or style, that on this dogma there could be no compromise, no fuzziness, no room for different opinion. You either believed in the Trinity or you were not a Christian, she stated. This was followed by a tortuous and completely incomprehensible attempt to explain the inexplicable, in the course of which she made it plain that Jews and Muslims have a less than full understanding of God because the Trinity is not a part of their dogma.

I respect the traditionalist Christian who can believe in the Trinity but, in spite of pondering it for years, I cannot. In any case, my wife had to gently restrain me from interrupting the service to ask a few relevant questions: Did the curate think Jesus believed in the doctrine of the Trinity? On what evidence, biblical or other? Did he in fact ever require a creedal belief from anyone? Did St. Paul, who never mentions it either? St. Paul, in fact, makes it plain in several places that however highly he thought of Christ he was definitely subordinate to God. As he bluntly says in I Corinthians 15:28 "Then shall the Son also be subject unto Him that put all things under Him, that God may be all in all." Did she know that the doctrine of the Trinity is not to be found explicitly in the Testament at all? Did she realize that the verse in Matthew which talks about baptizing all nations "in the name of the Father, and of the Son and of the Holy Ghost" is a later addition to the text? The New Testament elsewhere (in Acts) tells us clearly that the original Christian baptismal formula was baptism into the name of Jesus only. In fact, the earliest Christian mark of allegiance to Christ was simply the ability to say "Jesus is Kurios (Lord)." This, at any rate for the first Jews who became Christians, meant that Christ and not Caesar was their master, teacher or guru. It was by no means a statement about Jesus being God.

Recently, because of our difficulties in worshipping God in the midst of all the page-finding and other activities required by the contemporary Anglican service – never mind sermons which frequently insult one's intelligence – we have begun going occasionally to a Quaker Meeting House for Sunday service. The rough benches are on four sides and face in towards an old-fashioned wood stove. About twenty people attend and the main point of the meeting is to sit in silence for an hour meditating on the "inner light." Sometimes one or more members will stand and give a very brief insight or meditative reflection as the Spirit moves them. Otherwise, the silence is deep and the sense of God's presence is profound. Quakers, apart from a courageous commitment to active pacifism, to social service, and the belief that there is "that which is of God" in everyone, an inner light to be sought after and followed, have no creeds or dogmas. They are followers of Christ but require no assent to specific beliefs about his person. In other words, there is an openness and an acceptance of differences that is as refreshing as cool, clear water. Yet, there is a great sense of having the most important things in common, a spiritual journey and a commitment to peace and justice on the earth. This is solid stuff, but in the special sense I have been discussing here, it's a wonderfully fuzzy faith.

I am not suggesting we all become Quakers. But it is no accident that their deep commitment and witness to non-violence goes in tandem with their remarkably open stance with regard to who can be a Christian. The either-or logic of the past has always had strong overtones of violence. From the Crusades and Inquisition to the crude ousting of controversial Roman Catholic theologians from their teaching posts today; from the frequency with which the Church has blessed war down the ages to the violent tendencies of religiously based militias in the United States at this moment, the harsh legacy of the "we alone know and possess the truth" syndrome can be clearly discerned. The kind of tolerance which alone can make the world safe for all to dwell in will never be achieved until the prevailing religious ethos for all faiths and all spiritual seekers becomes fuzzier, becomes less dogmatic, more humbly aware of the infinite Mystery of the being of God.

7

The Role of Dreams

♀

Many traditional believers today are suspicious – indeed almost paranoid – about the so-called New Age movement. I say so-called because when you examine its leading ideas many of them are very old indeed. You can remain critical of some of these concepts, however, without foolishly missing the challenge being presented here. Tragically, for the churches, many of the facets of the New Age movement's appeal are precisely those that have always belonged to the heritage of the major religions but have been almost completely forgotten or ignored. Spiritual healing is one example. Another is the practice of meditation.

Dreams, however, and their power to reveal the deepest promptings of the divine Spirit within have been the subject most neglected by organized religion today. Paradoxically, their role in the foundation scriptures of Judaism, Christianity, and Islam is absolutely central and constant. For example, dreams are consistently seen as the source and means of divine revelation – the voice of God – in the great stories of both the Old and the New Testaments. You have only to reread Genesis, Matthew or Acts to see what I mean. In modern terms, they are what Freud called "the royal road to the unconscious." For all of us, since the unconscious is the place where the deepest wellsprings of our being flow, dreams constitute the medium through which "the still, small voice" of God can often be heard. Their importance for our spiritual life and growth can be enormous.

Significantly, as psychoanalysts have insisted for many years, the language of dreams is usually that of symbolism. Failure to understand that is a key reason why for so many their dreams remain largely irrelevant. As with religion itself, a purely literal approach to important dreams misses their real spiritual purpose. Consider the following story.

At lunch one day, a friend who is a highly successful businessman began telling me about a recurring dream he was having. Though the details varied every time he dreamed it, there were some persistent motifs. In all of them he was playing squash, either solo or with a faceless partner. In all of them he was fiercely competitive and determined to win. The strange thing, however, was that each time he had the dream he found the task of winning more difficult because of various obstacles placed in his way. In one dream, there were pieces of furniture strewn about haphazardly on the court. In another, he found himself using a baseball bat instead of a racquet. On the night before our lunch he had found himself trying to play using a hammer to strike the ball.

It has been my experience, confirmed by reading and by interviewing some experts in the field, that while many dreams are meaningless, simply a form of mental knitting or playing while we are asleep, those which stand out vividly, particularly if they are repeated, are trying to tell us something vital for our lives. The key to understanding them lies partly in knowing where the dreamer is at that moment – what's really going on in her or his life – and partly on seeing how the symbolism being used by the unconscious "fits" the person's own character and needs. In the case of my friend I was tempted, after some reflection, to venture an opinion as to the dream's meaning. (Incidentally, this is not my usual practice. I have no formal training in psychoanalysis, and few things are more likely to be off the mark than an amateur's attempts to interpret somebody else's dream life. Indeed, most analysts themselves admit there can be more than one valid understanding of any dream. In the end, with or without help, one has to see the meaning for oneself).

Brought up by a strict father whose motto could be summed up as "never walk when you can run," my friend is obsessed with competition and with winning. Even in his hobbies – skiing, racing in his several sailboats, and reading philosophy – he tends toward extremes. In business, though highly ethical, the same approach guides every endeavour. Since he is now nearing retirement, with no let-up in energy or ambition, it seemed evident to me that his inner self might be serving up a warning. Playing squash with a hammer is not only foolish, it is highly risky both to oneself and to others. In other words, his higher self was saying it was time for him to look at his life and where he was going. His excessive competitiveness was a flaw to be examined. The course he was on could be highly dangerous to his well-being and that of those nearest him.

I cite this example because there are millions of people who will tell you either that they never dream or that, if they do, they never remember them. Besides, they usually add, they're unimportant anyway. Since I felt this way for many years myself, I have a lot of sympathy for this point of view. But, I have come to believe that it's a major mistake.

I began taking notice of my own dreams after reading the works of Dr. Carl Jung for the first time. Surprisingly, once I started to pay attention to them, it became easier to recall them. As the Canadian analyst and author Marion Woodman once told me in a television interview, it's a little like a timid deer who, alert for danger, just sticks its nose into the clearing. Once it sees it will be safe there, it comes out more boldly into the open. At intervals, coinciding with significant moments in my life, I observed that some of my dreams had an almost luminous quality and were either confirming a recent decision or were counselling me in what path to take. At times I have felt like Jung did when he said he sometimes could hardly wait to go to sleep at night to see what lay in store. Because the language of dreams is always highly symbolic, and the obvious, surface meaning is scarcely if ever the correct one, it can take a number of weeks before the true significance of a dream becomes apparent. In some cases, it has taken me many months to discern their meaning, and there are one or two highly charged (and I am certain highly significant) dreams I'm still mulling over and waiting to unravel. As Jung warned, you have to "stay with the dream." You must scrutinize every detail, especially how it begins and how it ends, if you want it to yield its secrets.

As an example, here is one dream which helped me greatly at the time and which still throws light on my spiritual journey:

I found myself at the mouth of a large cave, high on the side of a mountain. In the valley below I could see charming alpine-like villages teeming with life. In the cave with me were two other adults, my parents, and in the floor of the cave there was a pool of crystal-clear water with a fair-sized trout swimming in it. I became aware that the fish was hungry and discovered at the same time that I had a loaf of bread – a kind of French stick – under my arm. I began breaking pieces off it and throwing them for the fish to eat. It devoured them greedily and obviously wanted more. I obliged and, as I watched with fascination, it began to grow. It was quickly outgrowing the pool and yet it still wanted more of the rapidly diminishing loaf. Suddenly, I became angry as I realized that the fish was intent on eating all the bread, leaving nothing for me. I told it, "No more," and, heading out of the cave, started the long climb down to the valley and the people there.

By itself, the dream means little. Certainly at the time, in spite of its vivid detail, it conveyed nothing comprehensible to me. Much later, though, during an hour-long interview in a series I hosted on Vision TV, Canada's interfaith network, called "Harpur's Heaven and Hell," I decided to tell the dream and take the risk of an unrehearsed, on-air analysis. My guest was the dream analyst the late Fraser Boa, author of *The Way of the Dream* and the maker of the twenty-hour film series of the same name which features the renowned dream psychoanalyst, Dr. Marie Louise von Franz, a colleague of Jung's.

Boa suggested that the fish probably stood for the intellectual and spiritual side of my personal makeup. The water symbolized consciousness and the possibility of a change in it. The bread represented my energy or life force. The parents who watched but said nothing represented the forces of past authority, superego, and resistance to any proposed change. According to him – and he simply suggested it for my reflection since, of course, the dreamer is the one who finally has to grasp the real meaning – there I was in a spot high and removed from the real action going on below in the villages of life; I was busily engaged in over-feeding the spiritual and academic side of myself to the neglect and risk of all else. What was important was that, at least at the unconscious level, I was deciding to stop and "come down" to engage in more practical living in the "real" world.

I found that insight particularly helpful because it made sense of the considerable tension and inner conflict I had been going through at the time I had had the dream in 1970. At the time I had been wrestling with my sense of vocation. In a certain sense, everything was going my way. I was Professor of New Testament and Greek at my old theological college, a position my father had always urged me towards. I had been there for six years, had tenure, long vacations in the summer to write or travel, and a commodious if ancient apartment in the college for my family and myself. After seven years in a busy, suburban parish, it seemed like an enviable position. What's more, I enjoyed teaching and was, I believe, reasonably good at it. But I was restless and unhappy. As I have said elsewhere, much of theological college life seemed inward-turned and remote from ordinary people and their real concerns. I felt that a great deal of what went on at the college was the Church busily talking to itself. Beyond the college walls, the world was being torn apart by the war in Vietnam and the opposition to it but we seemed blind to it or above it all.

Convinced that religion in general and Christianity

in particular were wrong in not using the mass media to communicate their message, I had already made a tentative sortie into the world of open-line radio, hosting a program also called "Harpur's Heaven and Hell" on a country and western station, CFGM in Richmond Hill, Ontario. As well, I had begun to write occasional opinion pieces for the *Toronto Star*'s weekly religion page (my first was headlined "The Gospel According to James Bond"), and I was a regular panellist on the CBC-TV Sunday morning show "Would You Believe?". Gradually, deep down, I was becoming aware that I really felt more at home in these various "hobbies" than teaching Greek and the New Testament to seminarians. But the inner parental voice inside kept saying, "You're called to be a minister. You spent ten years at university for an academic career in the Church. You can't throw all that away; God wouldn't like it."

The result was inner confusion and some depression. Then, when the position of religion editor at the *Toronto Star* became vacant early in 1971, a strong voice inside me urged me to take a chance and apply for it. The idea attracted me powerfully but frightened me half to death at the same time. What would my colleagues think? What would family (my father had died in 1968) and the Church authorities think? What about my former professors and all those who had always predicted I would one day be head of my old college or a bishop? Would I be able to do the job when I had never been to journalism school and when my academic specialty was ancient languages and the Bible? These and a thousand other fears assailed me.

It was during this period that I dreamed about the cave and the fish. Though I hadn't a clue then what it meant, I now feel it still gave me the strength and determination to act on its inner meaning. I "came down" from my academic and religious mountain to communicate spiritual, ethical and religious ideas to ordinary people in Canada's largest newspaper. Though I was on probation for the first three months (union rules) and at first I didn't even know where to find a pencil sharpener in the *Star* newsroom, it was undoubtedly the best and most liberating – but nevertheless traumatic – decision I had ever made. A few months later, having settled into my new career, I was on my way to cover the October 1971 Synod of Bishops in Rome. That was the first of many visits there over the next twelve years and the beginning of a (to me now) quite incredible list of foreign assignments all over the world.

Part of the function of dreams is to warn us of impending danger, a wrong course of action, or an imbalance in our personality. Here again, one always has to beware of taking the easiest and most obvious meaning. The language of dreams, I must stress again, is symbolism and it rarely yields its secrets easily or all at once. For example, many people, especially in their middle years, dream of dying and death. Only rarely, and always depending upon a host of factors related to what is going on in the life of the dreamer at that moment, do these signify that there is an immediate risk of dying. The purpose of dreams about death, when they occur to people who are more or less healthy and at the peak of their powers, seems to be that of the ancient Latin aphorism *memento mori*, "remember that you are mortal." In other words, should we be deliberately repressing or ignoring the fact that one day we are going to die, should we be behaving in a way that is really an attempt to deny our mortality – refusing so much as even to think about our own death, living more youthfully than is reasonable, or distracting ourselves from any serious spiritual thoughts whatever, by work, pleasures or other diversions – then often our unconscious will, so to speak, take us by the scruff of the neck and, through a vivid dream or even a nightmare, force us to confront the fact of our own eventual death. The unconscious always has our well-being in mind.

I have not found the many popular books which purport to tell you the significance of dream symbols or dream patterns of any use whatever in seeing the significance of either my own or other people's dreams. Quite the reverse, in fact. They actually hinder rather than help. This is because of the uniqueness of each personality together with the uniqueness of the web of circumstances in which each of us is entangled. With an ingenuity and fecundity surpassing all our ability to predict, our unconscious mind uses imagery specifically tailored and shaped to fit only us. However, it may help to know that in general dreams involving water may relate to our consciousness and changes needed there or that the fish is an ancient symbol for spirituality (and, of course, for Christianity); dreams about one's car not going or one's house being violated may refer to something going on in our lives that directly affects our energy flow or our bodily health; but it all depends on so many other variables. There is, at least in my experience, no short cut or easy route to take here. Understanding my own dreams has been very hard work, I have found. Apart from Boa's analysis of my dream I have never had the luxury of a psychoanalyst explaining them to me. As hinted already, even those who have had extensive psychoanalysis will tell you that it's not the analyst's job to sit and tell you what your dreams mean. He or she doesn't really know either. Only the client can see and "feel" the final application, and this takes some tough mental effort, not to mention the moral courage to do something about it once the meaning seems clear.

THE MAN WHOSE HOUSE WAS ON FIRE

A single man in my circle of friends and acquaintances, who had just turned forty, began having a recurring dream which left him frightened and shivering with perspiration every time he had it. He confided it to my wife and me one evening over coffee. He told how, while the details always varied considerably each time, the central theme was always the same. In the dream, he was sleeping in his own bed in his own home when suddenly he would realize with enormous panic that fire had broken out some-where and he was powerless to move or to escape. At first, taking a literal approach, he felt perhaps he was being warned to make sure his home was fireproof. He double-checked his smoke-alarm system. He moved furniture to make certain his path to both the front and the side doors would be clear in the event of fire. He became hyper-careful about cooking and any-thing even remotely related to the possibility of a fire hazard. Still the dream recurred and he was at risk of becoming completely paranoid about fire. He could scarcely get to sleep at night for fear both of the dream and of the reality to which he believed it pointed. Since he had a history of illness, and since, as I have said, dreams in which one's home is part of the symbolism often (but not always) are concerned in some way with one's body or physical existence, it seemed to me that the dream was not about a literal fire in a house but about some possibly serious threat to his health and well-being. He said he would work with the idea but he was not convinced. Some months later, he became very ill with a complicated form of pneumonia. Blood tests were done and to his great shock and dismay he was discovered to be HIV-positive. The pneumonia was actually the first step in a transition to being diagnosed with AIDS. A year and a half later, after a couple of months of acute suffering – borne with incredible courage and quiet, uncomplaining patience – he died.

THE DREAM OF AN ABANDONED BABY

Often, I have found that when we really need it, the unconscious sends us a dream of encouragement and insight. Of course, often it doesn't, or if it does, we don't recall it well enough to get the message. One time recently, however, a dream about a lost baby (of all things!) was of enormous assistance to me. Since my writing deals with extremely sensitive issues, and since my approach takes me well beyond the bounds of orthodoxy, I am frequently the target of criticism and anger from ultra-conservative quarters. As the Latin proverb well puts it, *odium theologicum pessimum* (there's no anger like religious anger). I regularly receive mail – much of it unsigned – offering threats, abuse and various forms of condemnation. Sometimes there will be a veritable torrent of what can only be called hate in the name of God and righteousness. Usually, it doesn't bother me. I expect criticism and disagreement. But, at times, when the anger is not about ideas but descends to name-calling and charges that I am "destroying the faith" or worse, it can wear me down. The dream I'm about to describe came at just such a moment. I felt angry and depressed at what I thought was a particularly unfair onslaught on my motives and my entire attempt to make faith relevant to people today.

Here is the dream:

I found myself wandering across open country much like the fields where I walk each morning before beginning my working day. There was a town or city barely visible on the horizon. Suddenly, I noticed a small bundle at the foot of a tree. I rushed over to look at it and it turned out to be a very young baby. It seemed obvious to me it had been either lost or abandoned and I picked it up determined to find the parents. At that instant, I heard strange sounds coming from the direction of the distant houses. There were a couple of police helicopters circling about overhead and I began to see a crowd of people engaged in some kind of search. Immediately, with the infant in my arms, I began running towards them and shouting: "The baby's here and it's okay." To my total consternation and alarm, the leaders of what now seemed to be a mob began crying out that the baby was indeed with me but that I was the one who had stolen it. As they got within range, they suddenly began throwing stones at me. I yelled to warn them they were going to hit the baby too, but they were so angry at what I allegedly had done that they kept throwing the rocks anyway. My last thought before the dream ended was that they didn't really give a damn about the baby.

Now, inasmuch as the point at which a dream ends can be the best clue, in my experience, to getting at the meaning, I began there. After sifting through the details in odd moments over the next few days, I woke up to what was being said. I saw that, while the image of a baby is a symbol for newness, creativity and the like, its meaning in this dream was something else. The overwhelming feeling I recalled was just how infinitely precious and vulnerable the baby seemed when I held it in my arms. Like the proverbial light bulb going on, I saw in a flash that in the dream it symbolized religious or spiritual truth. The people who were proclaiming most loudly that it belonged to them didn't in fact care deeply about it at all. They were more interested in attacking one whom they perceived as an enemy than in finding or protecting the truth itself. Others may interpret the symbolism differently. I can only say it "worked" for me. It enabled me to jettison the weight of lassitude and self-doubt that had been niggling at me and to throw myself with fresh vigour into my writing.

Like many, perhaps most, people, I sometimes dream of someone who has died a while ago. In earlier times, and still today among Aboriginal peoples – who have a much more immediate sense of their link with those who have gone before than we do – such dreams have been and are taken as evidence of survival beyond the grave. In my research for *Life After Death* in the late 1980s, I heard from many people who said that the force and clarity of their dreams of loved ones who had died were so unusual they convinced them that these persons were indeed alive on some different plane of being and had really conversed with them. Naturally, this was extremely reassuring and comforting to them. In my own case, the closest person to me to have died is my father. Since his sudden death in the fall of 1968, at age sixty-two, he has appeared occasionally in my dreams, and I too would say that the quality or "feel" of the dream has stood out from the ordinary, often garbled flow of events which usually stream through our minds while sleeping. He always seems very vital and at his peak of mental and spiritual energy. My belief that he is indeed alive in another dimension does not depend on such nocturnal encounters, but they have enlivened and strengthened it enormously.

I would like one day to undertake a study of dreams in the Bible. As I mentioned earlier, they play a remarkable part in both the Hebrew scriptures and the Greek New Testament. It's perhaps fitting to close this chapter by commenting briefly on my favourite. It's in Genesis 28:10-16 and is the well-known episode in the life of the patriarch Jacob (later called Israel) when he dreamed of a ladder between heaven and earth. First of all, here is the heart of the narrative itself: "And Jacob went out from Beer-sheba and went toward Haran. And he lighted upon a certain place, and tarried there all night because the sun was set; and he took of the stones of that place, and put them for his pillows, and lay down in that place to sleep. And he dreamed, and behold a ladder set up on the earth, and the top of it reached to heaven; and behold the angels of God ascending and descending upon it. And, behold, the Lord stood above it, and said, I am the Lord God of Abraham thy father, and the God of Isaac: the land whereon thou liest, to thee will I give it, and to thy seed; And thy seed shall be as the dust of the earth . . . and in thee and in thy seed shall all the families of the earth be blessed. And, behold, I am with thee, and will keep thee in all places whither thou goest, and will bring thee again into this land; for I will not leave thee, until I have done that which I have spoken to thee of. And Jacob awaked out of his sleep, and he said, Surely the Lord is in this place; and I knew it not."

Since, as we have seen, circumstances give the symbols in a dream their true meaning, it's important to know that Jacob (whose name in Hebrew means one who tricks or supplants another) was a real "mamma's boy" and that, having wronged Esau his brother at his mother's prompting, he had now been urged by her to flee for his life to her brother at Haran. Esau, she said, was "purposing to kill thee." So, the context was that he found himself hunted, alone at nightfall, in the middle of the vastness of the desert wilderness. It was an apparently God-forsaken spot and he was deeply afraid. Suddenly his unconscious breaks in with the dream. The place is not God-forsaken. Quite the contrary, in fact. This place and this time in his life are actually alive with revelation. There is communion or intercourse between the realm of the natural and that of the Spirit, symbolized by the angels moving on the ladder between the two orders. God is there at the centre of his fear and loneliness with promises of future blessing and present help. Jacob's consciousness is instantly raised to a wholly new level – "God was in this place and I knew it not." He is surprised to find the very opposite of all his worst expectations. He decides to call the place Bethel, meaning "the house of God."

When I said it was my favourite, it's because while I would not even begin to claim to have had anything similar in my own dream experiences, I have found the essence of Jacob's dream of great spiritual comfort all my life. If, on looking back, we can truly say of a particular crisis that God was surely in it though we didn't know it at the time, then it is entirely possible, some would say certain, that he is or will be in the midst of any crisis or difficulty to come. I find that a basis for hope.

8

Reaching Children With Spiritual Values

♀

The old New England saying "You can't do business from an empty wagon" comes to my mind whenever the urgent concern arises of how we are to pass on spiritual values and insights to the next generation. Many parents who find this question so painful are aware that the chief reason it is such a problem for them is that their own spiritual "wagon" is bare. They can't really do what they feel is required because they don't have any secure spiritual moorings or markers themselves. The faith they were raised in has faded and nothing solid has taken its place.

A clear sign of growing concern among parents over this issue is the sudden popularity in both the United States and Canada of religious schools. A story in the *Toronto Star* on July 22, 1995, headed, "Faithless Flocking to Religious Schools," described how in both countries Christian, Jewish and Muslim schools have seen a large influx of children from non-religious homes. About 13 per cent of students at

Roman Catholic schools in the United States, for example, are not Roman Catholic. At Orthodox Jewish schools in the States, where study of Torah and Hebrew is mandatory, nearly one-third of the students come from non-observant Jewish homes. Parents who are not religious themselves nevertheless want their children to develop spiritual and moral values. Increasingly, they worry that the public schools are not able to assist them in this.

In my days as a minister in a growing suburban parish there were always a few of what we called the "Sunday School dumpers." These were parents who (sometimes still in pyjamas) would drop off their children for Sunday School and then come back later to fetch them. They had little or no use for church themselves but felt it was "good" for their little ones. Today, with perhaps more honesty – or is it partly an even greater indifference than then? – most parents don't go even that far. The result in many Western countries has been that unless parents specifically send their children to either public or private religious schools and colleges, their children get no formal religious or spiritual instruction whatever. Consequently, today we have the first generation of young people in North America and Europe who are for the most part ignorant of the religious traditions in which their own parents were raised. Knowledge of the Bible, for example, is all but nonexistent. The implications of this have yet to be fully calculated.

What are we to do about this? Forcing children to go to religious services or classes against their will is obviously no answer. Forced spirituality ultimately is no spirituality at all and will quickly be renounced or ignored once the child comes of age. Taking them with you to church, synagogue or temple is obviously a much better route. Indeed, in many cases, even in times of declining religious observance such as now, the arrival of children moves people back to the religious institutions of their own youth. "A little child shall lead them." But, unless the return is undertaken with sincerity and real commitment by the parents, it too is ultimately a stopgap measure. As soon as they are old enough to discern how much the organized religion truly means to their elders, the children will see through any charade and act accordingly themselves.

What this means, then, is that before worrying about the spirituality of their children adults have to begin to provide for their own. This cannot be stressed enough. The only genuine spiritual heritage parents themselves can provide is that which really matters to them in their own lives. The lived example, the ethos of the home, the values honoured not by word but by the way time, talent and money are spent, the day-to-day life style and the common goals of the family unit – these are what determine what will be passed on in the end. Children have an uncanny knack of seeing past all our pretence and polite veneer to the reality beneath. They internalize for good or ill what they know to be the truth of the home in all its facets.

One cardinal truth stands out. Children are innately spiritual. They have a natural spiritual capacity and aptitude for trust, for truth, for beauty and for justice. In a profound sense, each child is a potential spiritual genius. When we think a child has a natural bent for music or for sport, we are prepared to do anything within our power to further that gift. For example, our neighbours across the street have two sons who like hockey and, though both are still in elementary school, have already attained considerable proficiency as players. I see their father out in the bitterest of winter weather cleaning the ice on the lake for their rink, getting up at all hours of the morning to drive them to various games and practices, spending endless time showing them how best to shoot the puck, make body checks and all the rest. He's determined to do all he can to help them one day play in the National Hockey League as professionals. If more parents had the vision of their children's spiritual potential and fostered it with anything like this kind of devotion, a remarkable transformation could occur over time.

To put it rather more theologically for a moment, consider this: the Christian tradition has always had at its core the concept that God's Word or Logos, God's highest self-expression, became enfleshed or incarnate at the birth of Jesus Christ. When you go beyond the literal text and plumb the deeper meaning of the myth, however, you find that what is really being said is that humanity has become a vehicle for the divine. As the beginning of John's Gospel says, the Logos that became flesh in Jesus Christ was "the true light which lighteth every man that cometh into the world." In other words, every baby that is born bears the light of God within, is an expression of the divine Word. Other faiths put the same sublime truth in other terms. Hinduism, for example, teaches that "thou art that" – meaning the divine Atman or breath of God is within every soul. Such an understanding of our spiritual nature throws the whole task of passing values and spiritual truths into a completely fresh light. If we approach teaching our children from this perspective, we will never have to worry either about their developing a strong sense of self-worth or their having the inner resources to cope with life's opportunities and disappointments. The seeds of a strong sense of social justice are to be found in this perspective as well. Once a child sees himself or herself as a Spirit-bearer or full child of God, the realization that this is also true of others provides the foundation for loving one's neighbour as oneself.

Over the years, it has become more and more evident to me that the kind of God people believe in as adults flows directly from the kind of people their parents or parent-substitutes were. We may, even as grown men and women, think of God intellectually in one way and yet, at an unconscious level, feel about God in a totally different manner because of our childish understandings. Millions of people, no matter what their official creed or lack of one may be, carry deep within themselves very powerful concepts of God as a tyrannical, vindictive or capricious despot – or perhaps a cruel absence. They can never come to a living, committed trust in the Creator because these false concepts, transmitted in earliest childhood, still reverberate within. We have to face these harmful inheritances and then consciously let them go. Parents in the end will do more to shape their children's understanding of God by what they do and say than by any formal teaching. It's a solemn responsibility but it's also a remarkable opportunity.

Obviously, the earliest months and years are the most crucial for the development of the child. I agree with those who are experts in child-rearing and early nurture when they state that by the time a child is three years old the parents will already have done more than half of what is truly lasting in all that they will ever do. The amount of love and acceptance given at this critical period will always manifest itself later in proper self-esteem, capacity for trust, and the ability to relate compassionately to others. Though it seems obvious, it cannot be emphasized too much. If you truly want the best for your children, if you want them to realize their full potential as human beings and be aware of their own spiritual riches from their earliest days, surround them with consistently loving care. Let them know that they are loved not just by you but also by a loving God who is within them and around them and in the whole of creation.

I have baptized hundreds of babies in the past and believe that, even when it is done more as a social ritual (the majority of cases) than as a serious religious act, it is a powerful sign and symbol of the fact that every child, Christian or non-Christian, is a fresh expression of the Creator. Yet, I have to honestly say that there are aspects of the baptismal service in all Christian denominations practising infant baptism that I personally find offensive or unhelpful. I believe sin is an important reality and certainly not to be dropped from our moral thinking about life. But, to burden a newborn child with all the heavy talk about its sin, as is done for example in the Anglican service, and to go on about his or her now being enlisted in the fight against "sin, the world, and the devil," is hardly an upbeat welcome into the human family and the cosmos. I suggest to those parents who are going to follow the traditional baptism with their children – or as an alternative for those who don't intend to – that you consider an additional simple ceremony in your own home or out of doors. We could borrow from the way various North American Indian tribes welcomed, and in some cases still welcome, newborns into the world. Instead of talk of sin and evil, the child is told that the four winds, the lakes and rivers, the sun and the stars joyfully join in welcoming him or her. I leave it to the imagination of the reader to improvise on similar themes and create an appropriate, simple ritual all your own. It makes spiritual sense to me that we place our children firmly in the story of the earth and of nature. Surely teaching children about nature and their part in it is a vital task for all parents.

The greatest danger of all for children and young people is to grow up in a spiritual vacuum. As spiritual beings, this kind of emptiness within is an open invitation for false gods – mindless, materialistic consumerism, addictions of various kinds, or wanton destructiveness and violence. It is not surprising that the decline of organized religion has been accompanied by the proliferation of sects and cults. There are reportedly some five thousand cults today in North America alone. Nor is this uniquely a problem in the West. Now that Shoko Ashara and six of his disciples in the Aum Shinri Kyo religious sect in Japan have been arrested and charged with murder (June 5, 1995) in the terrorist-style gas attacks on the Tokyo subway, much soul-searching is going on there about the reasons so many university students from the best colleges found his teachings attractive. Reiko Hatsumi, a Japanese author, wrote a piece in the May 24 *New York Times* in which he said that Japan lacks something most other cultures have: established religions that have stood the test of time and offer a moral standard. (Even if one deviates from this standard one knows it is there.) "Shinto has no code of ethics or dogma," he said. Buddhism in Japan has degenerated into a set of rites for burials. "In this spiritual vacuum, any new religion can creep in and find nourishment, however fraudulent."

Hatsumi noted that the breakdown of the extended family and formidable pressures on children to get ahead in an overcrowded, highly competitive society have meant that many children in Japan have little to inspire them or to look forward to. "So, when someone like Mr. Ashara comes along and takes time to listen and to give advice that seems to resolve dilemmas and solve problems, the young hand over their hearts and follow." During the 1970s, when I was reporting on religion for the *Toronto Star*, whenever I investigated offbeat North American religious sects and cults attracting young people I observed similar forces at work. The young were finding within cults the meaning, relationships and disciplines that were all sadly lacking in their homes. When anxious parents came to my office, as they did from time to time, loudly demanding exposés and crusades to free their teenager from this or that guru's grip, I quickly saw in nearly every case why the cult had proven to be more attractive to the young person than her or his family. Of course some religious movements and groups can be dangerous. But it is naive to suppose that it isn't just as risky to leave our youth to the overall sense of alienation and despair that being at the disposal of "market forces" alone inevitably brings.

I have the opportunity occasionally to speak to large groups of high school students about spiritual themes. They seem genuinely astounded when instead of beginning with quotes from the Bible or other traditional religious texts I take them to the world of modern physics. It seems to me that science today offers the most alluring road to thinking about God and one's place in the universe and I have found that young people are hungry to follow it. At the same time, one can help them enormously by being able to point out the limitations of science to them. They need and want to know that there are other valid ways of understanding life and themselves. I bring to their attention such books as *The Universe Is a Green Dragon* by physicist Brian Swimme (Bear Books) or *The Story of the Universe* by Thomas Berry (Harper and Row).

They seem equally pleasantly surprised when I go on to show how the environmental movement – about which most young people feel keenly – is at its core a spiritual movement. The whole issue of the human-earth relationship and its essentially spiritual character cannot be too highly stressed when attempting to bridge the communication gap with teenagers and young adults. The same is true when it comes to the issues of global peace and the quest for justice on behalf of the oppressed – from poverty-stricken peasants in poorer parts of the Third World to Aboriginal peoples everywhere. Youthful idealism is a wonderful thing but unless it is linked to some powerful spiritual roots and insights, which gives it an organized worldview and a focused vision for the future, it can quickly dissipate and eventually lead to cynicism. They want and need a spirituality that is not "me in my small corner" or "safe in the arms of Jesus" but instead is adventurous, relevant and demanding.

Parents can be of the most help to children and teenagers by encouraging as early as possible an ongoing, open dialogue about God, moral and aesthetic values, meaning and purpose. If your own understanding of spirituality is that of an ongoing process in which questioning, doubt and growth belong together, then the young feel free rather than coerced to make their way. This dialogue doesn't need a special time or venue. It can take place over the dinner table, in the car, after seeing a particular video or television program, or whenever the opportunity arises. A basic rule of teaching applies: move from the known to the unknown. First get a common "coinage" by talking about some shared experience or awareness and move from that to deeper issues. The important thing is not to adopt some heavy, now-we're-going-to-be-spiritual approach. Few things are likelier to cast a pall over the discussion than that!

Many parents who write to me say that, in despair of what passes for religious indoctrination in many Sunday Schools or their equivalent in other faiths, they have formed instruction or enquiry classes in one another's homes. Led by adults who are prepared to spend considerable time in learning and preparation themselves, these groups focus on exploring

religious and spiritual concepts in the spirit of dialogue mentioned above, avoiding the older-style,
didactic, down-from-on-high methods of the past.
There is a steady emergence today of similar discussion and exploration groups on spiritual themes for
adults, especially among the so-called baby-boomers.
Sometimes these groups are on the edges of established religious communities and regard their meetings as being complementary to them. Increasingly,
however, they are completely independent of any
organized religion. They're becoming a sort of under-
ground church of people who have realized that
while they can be spiritual on their own, it is easier
and much more effective when they are supported by
a community, however small. There is also a need for
rituals of some kind. Those who leave behind the
rituals of organized religion need to formulate more
relevant rituals of their own. I strongly recommend
Robert Fulgham's 1995 book, *From Beginning to End:
The Rituals of Our Lives*, for help in this regard.

There is no single, simple answer, then, to the
question with which we began: how do we transmit a
heritage of spiritual and moral values to the next generation? For some parents, it will mean a return to
established religious settings with a new point of view,
one that is less literal and that is prepared to ignore
aspects of the faith which no longer seem meaningful
or particularly well-founded. Their faith will no
longer be foisted willy-nilly upon their children but
be treated as an ongoing subject for discussion and

dialogue in the home. For others, the path will be far less orthodox. The home itself will be the primary spiritual source, supplemented perhaps by informal classes in concert with other like-minded parents. But in either case it will take hard work. The spiritual preparation of a child is the most important part of his or her entire education for living. Unless we see that and are ready to devote major time and other resources to it, we will fail them at the most crucial point of all.

Finally, a word about sex and sexual moral values. There is, I believe, a strong link between the excessive and exploitive attitude to sex in the Western world today – we truly live in a sex-saturated culture – and the overly negative and repressive approach to sex of the dominant religion, Christianity. What is repressed is always expressed sooner or later in a destructive manner. Some of the Church's motives in the past were undoubtedly benign. There was a wish to protect the family and to avoid the obvious pain associated with marital breakup, infidelity, promiscuity and all the rest. But some were self-serving, too. Much of the Church's obsession with sex – which is totally contrary to the documents in the Bible on which the Church is founded – flowed from a desire to control people at their most vulnerable point. This same desire for control can still be seen today in the continuing negative pronouncements of some major churches.

What has been sadly lacking has been a thoroughly positive theology of the body and of sexuality in general. As a result the prevailing message in the past was that sex is to be tolerated only if it is aimed at producing babies and is experienced with a minimum of enjoyment. In recent years, there have been some signs of progress towards a recognition of the spiritual rewards of a loving, committed sexual relationship quite apart from the procreation of children. But, as far as the young are concerned, the prevailing message from religion has been "don't." Everything in popular culture pressures them to see sex as the highest of all possible goods just at a time when their bodies are stirring with instinctual drives. Consequently, parental and religious strictures and warnings seem to be heavy, negative and, above all, out of touch with reality.

It helps them enormously if children are brought up in a warm, loving environment where their parents have a fully developed relationship at every level. The best sex education happens in the home where healthy sex is being lived rather than preached, where parents make sure their children realize, at each stage of their development, that their bodies are good, that their sexual feelings and drives are natural and good, and that God has a purpose for that aspect of their lives. Instead of instilling fears over becoming pregnant or causing a pregnancy, or over sexually transmitted diseases (although of course they need to know the simple facts here also), the approach should be positive. Young people need to know that values such as commitment, fidelity and, when appropriate, chastity are important to their own inner growth and integrity, and why. Without heavy-handedness, they can (and I believe they want to) learn how in sex much more than our physical nature is active, that our total being – body, mind and spirit – is involved. At its best, a fulfilling sexual relationship is a way of knowing the Divine Lover, a foretaste of union with God. We urge them to be careful with their sexuality not because it is sinful but because it is so great a gift.

9

So What? The Benefits of a Living Faith

Long ago, like anyone with the slightest interest in serious writing, I was told always to "write about what you know yourself." When it comes to the issues raised by the title of this chapter, this piece of wisdom is particularly relevant. This is not the place for abstract theories or second-hand descriptions. I promised at the outset that I would try to make this book as personal as possible and I will try to honour that commitment especially at this point.

The television evangelists and many preachers in Christian churches and in other faiths as well unabashedly declare that trust and belief in their vision of God is the key to health, happiness and material prosperity. Over the years, I have often interviewed religious celebrity figures who, rather than feeling embarrassment about their expensive clothes, cars and life styles – I always remember comedian Lenny Bruce's comment about being wary of "any man of God who has more than one suit" – were actually proud of them. They believed that conspicuous worldly success was a mark of God's special blessing. Their preaching (understandably) laid heavy emphasis on texts, taken out of context from the Bible, that promise that any giving "to the Lord's work" (to that particular evangelist) will come back tenfold.

This kind of it-pays-to-believe approach to spirituality is really a capitulation to a crude form of materialism in which real faith has been replaced by an attempt at magic. In magic, the approach is one of "if you do A and then B, C will of necessity be the result." There is no such formula in a living relationship with God. You enter it, you remain committed to it, not because it may be profitable in some way, but because you know it to be true. You are left no other choice because the truth itself compels you. It is this profound, deeply intuitive grasp of the fact that there is a loving Presence at the heart of life and of the universe itself who fuels our love and our belief in the midst of doubts or even despair. Once the truth of God's reality has been grasped, you begin to understand what the Psalmist meant when he said, "Even though He slay me yet will I trust Him." For countless prophets and others in the community of faith down the years, trusting in God has often brought not worldly success but suffering, persecution, and even death. The whole point of the Christian gospel is based upon a rejection of material, celebrity, or success-oriented values. For Jesus, it meant in the end a cross.

Suffering, from a purely human standpoint, is to be avoided at all costs and is frequently taken as a sign of "not making it" or even of having incurred the divine "wrath." But, in the life of the Spirit, suffering is often involved. Obedience to what we perceive as the will of God is seldom the easy path. All growth, as we have seen, inevitably involves some degree of pain. To put our trust in God is not – contrary to what many preachers repeatedly suggest – to be always free of depression, free of failure, free of anxiety and fear. As Paul, himself no stranger to weakness and suffering, once said: "We have this treasure in vessels of clay." We may live "in the Spirit" but our humanity remains and must be fully accepted.

My own experience of knowing God has involved times of darkness and uncertainty. There have been many dry periods when I was much more aware of the divine absence than the divine Presence. I do not go about with a perpetual hymn of praise on my lips or with constant joy in my heart. As all the great religious leaders remind us, no matter how close we may feel to God, life is difficult. It is also a mystery. Much happens to us and to others we will never fully understand on this plane of being at all.

That, of course, is not the whole story. While I have known and still experience difficulties, temptations, doubts and failures, my own humble experience has been that God makes good on the promise to be with us in "the valley of the shadow" even when we are feeling abandoned. While there are times of "dying," there are joyous times of resurrection, too. Sometimes we may feel deep empathy with T. S. Eliot's words about those "who are only undefeated because they have gone on trying." But, eventually, we find ourselves saying from the bottom of our heart the Psalmist's words: "I waited patiently for the Lord and He inclined unto me and heard my cry. He brought me up also out of an horrible pit, out of the miry clay, and set my feet upon a rock and established my goings. And He has put a new song in my mouth, even praise unto our God." (Psalm 40:1-3.)

As I said earlier, while pain or grief can seem almost unendurable at the time, afterwards, looking back, we can often see in those times that "the hand of God" was working. The times of spiritual growth in my life have usually not been those periods or occasions when everything seemed to be flowing along beautifully. Often we learn the most "the hard way." It may sound pious but it's true nonetheless. It is in the moments of weakness that we learn to rely upon the strength God alone can supply. It has been the weeks or months when he seemed most absent that God was, I believe, most active in my life.

I vividly remember one night early in my first year as an undergraduate at Oxford when I felt so homesick and so depressed by the thought of all the years of study I still had ahead of me in order to train for the ministry and an eventual academic career (I was to spend ten years at university in all) that I was very close to packing my bags and quitting. I realized it would be a disappointment and indeed a disgrace to turn my back on the Rhodes Scholarship I had won and to give up the great opportunity I had been given, but I just felt so unhappy and alone that deserting the ship seemed my only way out. Sad feelings that had been growing for weeks had turned to bleak despair. I was standing in the quadrangle at Oriel College and had actually decided to leave when the sound of the college organ floated out from the chapel. The organist had begun practising and by a strange chance was playing an old hymn much loved by my father. Suddenly, my eyes filled with tears and I realized I couldn't simply walk away from it all. I thought again of how my father, who never had the chance of a college education, had dreamed of my one day going to Oxford and of how hurt he would be by my abrupt departure and obvious loss of nerve. In a while, the organist went on to music I didn't know, but as I paced in the quad I seemed to hear a voice telling me I was to stay at my post, so to speak, and that I would be given the comfort and courage I so badly needed for the task of the three-year course ahead. I felt a surge of new hope and energy and I went to bed and slept well for the first time in weeks. Oxford turned out to be one of the best experiences of my life. I remain continually grateful that I decided, and was given strength, to stay the course.

However, if we are not guaranteed success, total health or constant bliss, what is gained by trusting in some ultimate reality we call God? A short answer is, everything. If we are committed to the God of love and mercy and infinite wisdom who made us for a relationship with him, everything radically changes. There is a reason and purpose to life beyond seeking pleasure, material prosperity or raising the next generation. There is meaning to the cosmos and our place in it. All that is beautiful in people, in nature, in literature, drama, music or art has an eternal significance. Death is no longer the end but the door to a much wider experience that holds the reasonable hope of being reunited with one's loved ones and of "knowing as we have been known." Suffering too has a meaning beyond itself. As we have seen, it can have a redemptive power. For those who open themselves to it, belief in such a God is not some peripheral idea to be used on Sundays or certain special occasions and then put in storage again. It becomes the anchor or foundation for everything else, every aspect of daily life. Everything from our most intimate relationships to our work and plans for the future take shape and fulfilment in its light. God becomes a moment-by-moment companion, the supreme confidant of all our days. The whole of life is seen in the light of eternity.

I would personally be unable to make any sense out of life whatever were it not for believing in and knowing the Creator behind and beneath all else. That belief eclipses all other facts in its luminosity and power. It infuses my life and work with hope. Otherwise, I would have to agree with Lord Bertrand

Russell, who counselled that "only on the firm foundation of unyielding despair can the soul's habitation henceforth be safely built." Russell, who was steeped in atheistic assumptions, was at least logical in his conclusion. Without God, there is ultimately only hopelessness. The universe is a mere fluke and we are the playthings of random evolutionary forces going finally nowhere. Belief in and trust in God do not magically solve every problem or remove all mystery. But, for me they make it possible to see the deeper patterns and meanings in my own life, in those of the people around me, and in the wider human community as it has moved through history. Particularly today, when we are being drowned in a deluge of information, my faith alone makes it possible for me to keep a footing and to have a place of reference from which to make sense of it all. One of the chief reasons for so much alienation and the widespread feeling of meaninglessness among young people today is the spiritual vacuum within them. Without more than perhaps a vague sense of "the Force" or some other First Mover, the youth have no principle of coherence to judge by, no firm ground on which to stand. And so they drift. Drugs, violence and sexual promiscuity all are attempts either to escape feeling meaningless or to impose a meaning where they can otherwise find none.

When I look back on the various turning points of my life, I am profoundly conscious of there having been a guiding hand, a grace totally beyond any personal merit or deserving. I have never known the kind of "do this" or "do that," moment-by-moment guidance claimed by many conservative Christians. Rather, I have frequently been very uncertain before making major decisions. But, in retrospect, I can see that they were steps of faith taken in the spirit of Abraham who, we are told, went out in obedience to a divine call, yet "not knowing whither he went." I can only marvel and give thanks for the way in which the Spirit was leading in it all. A seemingly chance remark by Miss McGregor, my wonderful English teacher in my first year of high school, led to my interest in learning Greek. I began taking lessons after school from a retired friend of hers, and eventually won a scholarship in Greek and Latin which paid my tuition for four years at the University of Toronto. The fact that I intended to study Classics or "Greats" at Oxford if chosen was, I believe, a major factor in my being selected as a Rhodes Scholar from Ontario in 1951. This made possible the three years at Oxford, something a person with my very ordinary background and limited family funds could never otherwise have aspired to.

Later, I felt guided in leaving parish work for seminary teaching, and then disillusionment with teaching led eventually to work on open-line radio, writing for the *Toronto Star* and a commitment to communicate spiritual ideas and values through the mass media. Whatever success I have been granted in this task has been by the Grace of God. Yes, I have worked as hard at it as I knew how because my understanding of grace is based upon that "fuzzy" concept of St. Paul's that you work as though it all depends on you and trust as though it all depends upon God. As we have seen, he put the paradox or fuzzy logic this way: "Work out your own salvation with fear and trembling for it is God that worketh in you."

None of this is written in the foolish belief that I am somehow more special or favoured than anyone else. That is the last thing I would want to claim. My only point here is to give personal substance to the more general conviction that when you seek to find and to know God, results do happen. The promise of Jesus that those who truly seek will find is very true. The Psalmist once issued this invitation: "Taste and see that the Lord is good." In many other passages in both the Old and New Testaments there is a similar open invitation to experience for ourselves the reality and joy of the divine Presence. For example, "Let him [or her] that is athirst come . . . and drink of the water of life freely." There is, in fact, a kind of dialectic to the life of faith. We take a step in commitment and trust. Experience then confirms that something real is happening and our hope grows stronger. We take another step and a pattern begins to emerge. It's not automatic. Sometimes we take a step or two backwards. But a body of experience begins to be built up. In the bleak times, the memory of how God has been good in the past is what keeps us going until the "light of His countenance" breaks forth once more.

The implications of a living trust in the Infinite Source of all wisdom, energy and light for our mental, emotional and physical health are, I'm convinced, not yet sufficiently understood and valued in our largely secular culture. There are no guarantees, of course. There are complex factors involved in human wholeness and health, from our heredity to the environment we live in. Yet, as Norman Cousins proves beyond any shadow of doubt in his important book *Head First*, and as I have attempted to document in *The Uncommon Touch*, having a foundation in our lives that gives us meaning, purpose, faith, hope and love is ultimately much more therapeutic than any amount of medical technology. Dr. Carl Jung discovered what most doctors today will confirm: the underlying causes of much human ill health flow from unresolved spiritual and emotional problems. Jung said that about two-thirds of the patients he saw needed more than anything else some spiritual basis or framework for their lives. It is my deep conviction that the greatest advances in healing lie ahead in the discovery of further ways in which the spiritual and the physical planes of existence relate to one another.

Some Final Thoughts

On Goodness

The *Atlantic Monthly*, December 1989, had a fascinating essay headed "Can We Be Good Without God?" I once debated the same issue on CBC Radio's national open-line show, "Cross Country Checkup." It's the sort of puzzle professional ethicists like to argue and theorize about. But it's not just a topic for academic games or intellectual magazines. It has great significance for our everyday living.

As my philosophy tutor drummed into me many years ago, it's important to look at any question critically before attempting to answer it. There's nothing wrong with the question "Can we be good without God?" but a closer look at it reveals that how you understand it has much to do with how it is to be resolved. On a straightforward, surface level, the answer must be an unqualified yes. We know it's possible for firm believers in God to be evil and to do evil things – any reading of Church history abundantly supports that conclusion and there are plenty of other examples. In this century alone, German soldiers in the Second World War wore belt buckles with the words "*Gott mit uns*" (God is on our side) inscribed on them, and the dominant religious community in South Africa used its version of Christian theology to shore up and maintain the racism of apartheid. I recently heard from a family of another race and faith living in a predominantly Anglo-Saxon, Christian area in Ontario whose lives have been made miserable by over-zealous true believers who'd like to "convert" them to their own version of "the truth." Tolerance is low on their scale of values. Yet at the same time, there are many good people, including atheists or agnostics, who never attend church, temple or synagogue. They include the young Canadian couple I met in India while visiting Calcutta to do a feature story on Mother Teresa. They were professed atheists working at their own expense in one of earth's saddest yet brightest places, the Home of the Dying. Jesus himself made it very plain that professions of faith are never enough by themselves. In the parable of the two sons who were asked by their father to go and work in his vineyard, it wasn't the one who made loud protestations of his obedience who was praised. It was the one who at first refused to go at all and yet ended up going and doing the work. The story makes plain that "doing the will of God" is more important than the ability to talk about it or to recite certain approved dogmas. Paul, in one of the sublimest passages in all literature – his "Hymn to Love" in I Corinthians 13 – says you can have faith that can move mountains and yet be nothing if you lack love. In fact, he specifically states that while faith, hope and love are the things that last forever, "the greatest of these is love."

Despite all of this, my answer to the question "Can we be good without God?" is a firm no. Obviously, then, I'm looking at more than the superficial sense of this query, the one that first strikes us. In the final analysis, I am convinced we can none of us be good – believers and unbelievers alike – without God. The Creator who makes the sun shine and the rain fall upon "the just and the unjust" alike without favour or discrimination is the foundation and source of all goodness wherever and in whomsoever it is found. Again one of my favourite Bible passages rings in my ears: "For, in Him we live and move and have our being." The loudest and cleverest of God-deniers is as much in the "hand" of God as anyone. Wherever goodness is found – often in the most unlikely hearts and places – God is there. Without God, I believe, there would be nothing at all.

At least one part of the original question, however, remains to be probed. When we ask, "Can we be good without God?" it's fair to ask a second question. What do we mean by "be good"? I don't think we mean being "goody-goody." As Plato pointed out nearly 2,500 years ago, being good has to do with realizing our ultimate purpose as human beings. What is the good for humans and what does it mean to be good were primary questions in classical times and still are today in many other cultures. But, goodness itself is unfortunately not much contemplated today in Western society. It's just assumed we know what we mean when we urge our children to live it or lament the lack of it in others. I believe we need to think and talk more about goodness in the media and elsewhere, and especially with children and young people.

Love is above and within goodness, as all major religions maintain, but the word love itself has been so weakened by our common usage as to be often unhelpful. True love is not passive and never merely sentimental. It combines compassion, honest and active willing of the good of others, and a commitment to personal and public justice in word and deed. Any spirituality that merely condones the status quo is seriously distorted. Personal goodness involves courage and integrity in regard to one's inner truth and to truth in general. It flows in those who properly love themselves yet, when appropriate, gladly put others first. For the person interested in living a life of faith and spirituality, it means becoming daily more the embodiment of what he or she was truly meant to be, a full co-worker with God. As Canadian newsman Peter Trueman used to say in an editorial at the end of his nightly television broadcasts, "That's not news, but that too is reality."

HYPOMONE

I have deliberately left one aspect out of this brief summary of goodness because it merits attention on its own: courageous perseverance. First, a short introduction. The man who said an atheist is a person who has "no invisible means of support" was once Governor General of Canada, Lord Tweedsmuir (1875-1940), who wrote novels under his given name, John Buchan. As a boy, I avidly read his books and was deeply influenced by them in later life also. His most popular novels were *Prester John*, *The Thirty-Nine Steps*, and *Sick Heart River*, but the one I liked most was *Mr. Standfast*, written in 1919. The novel celebrates the glory and grief of a quiet heroism. Standfastness – or endurance – a dogged determination to persevere or "see the thing through" no matter how hard or even agonizing the effort may be, is not popular these days. We generally prefer softer, less challenging virtues. In an age when almost everything computes or moves at the touch of a button, the idea of standing fast, of staying at one's post, of doing the mundane but necessary duty, of enduring the load for one more mile, holds little appeal for many people.

Oddly enough, the King James Version of the Bible – in spite of the splendour of its language – has served us badly here. In the Greek text, there is one word that comes ringing at you constantly all through the Pauline and other exhortations to live ethically. It's "*hypomone*," which the KJV always translates as patience. But, in contemporary English, patience doesn't have the clout that it had back in 1611. The meaning has changed to something rather mild. Indeed, some see patience as weakness. In the original Greek, *hypomone* is anything but weak or mild. The word is made up of two parts, *hypo*, meaning under, and *mone*, from the verb meaning to remain. Literally, then, *hypomone* means staying under a particular task or burden rather than fleeing it or tossing it off. In essence, it refers to a combination of courage and perseverance in the face of difficulties and the temptation to quit. Top athletes in any sport may not know the Greek word but they know the reality. So does anyone who has ever worked or trained to be really good at anything – playing an instrument, honing some other talent, or mastering a branch of learning. There is always a point – and often many – at which sheer weariness, or fear of failure, or a dozen other excuses whisper in our ear that it would be much simpler just to stop.

But, it's not just in relation to some specific duty or task that the need for *hypomone* or gutsy endurance presents itself. Life, as most of us know, can abruptly, for many reasons, oppress us or can slowly wear us down. For many people it's a major task just to keep on going on. Loved ones are suddenly taken from us; disappointments of every sort assail us; for one reason or another daily living loses its colour or taste and depression clouds our vision. That this is entirely normal does not make it any easier to bear. Today many thousands, perhaps millions, in the West are just hanging on by their fingernails. I could blame unemployment, alienation, the manifold stresses of urbanized living, or a myriad of other causes, but at bottom it's a more basic aspect of our human condition coming to the fore. Life is difficult. Trying to live a life of faith is difficult. Suffering of one sort or another is inevitable sooner or later for everyone. We need courage and the strength just to carry on. The worst thing you can do for your children or teens is to prevent them from having to face the harsher realities of existence. Not to acquire some *hypomone* early in life is to be set up for some very nasty surprises later on. But this kind of courage cannot come from an act of will alone. It comes to us more readily when we know that we are not alone; that there is a loving Presence around us and within us from whom we can gather the strength to endure and eventually to overcome any obstacle. There is a well-loved hymn that is singing in my head as I write this. It begins: "Immortal, Invisible, God only wise; In light inaccessible, hid from our eyes." Two verses seem particularly relevant:

> Fear not, He is with you, O be not dismayed,
> For He is thy God and will still give you aid.
> He'll strengthen you, help you and cause you to
>   stand,
> Upheld by His mighty, omnipotent hand.

When through the deep waters He calls you to
> go,
The rivers of woe shall not you overflow.
For, He will be with you your troubles to bless,
And sanctify to you your deepest distress.

THE POWER OF FORGIVENESS

Most people who recognize that life is ultimately about the nurture and shaping of our true, inner self, or soul, are deeply aware of the need for change. Only the fatted steer in its stall – or its human equivalent – could smugly feel it had already "arrived" at the journey's goal. That's why it's a good spiritual practice, not just on special occasions such as, for example, at each New Year, but frequently throughout the year as well, to take stock, make resolutions, and chart fresh courses for our lives. I suggest that as we do this each in our own way we should also take a fresh look at one of the most powerful of all the forces available for transforming our lives – forgiveness. There are very few spiritual qualities with greater potential to heal the wounds we incur in our physical, mental and emotional lives, not to mention its potential to enhance our relationships and our overall zest for life itself, than this one.

There's good reason forgiveness is featured at the heart of perhaps the best-known Christian prayer in the world, the Lord's Prayer taught by Christ to his disciples. But, it lies also at the inner core of Judaism,

Islam and other world religions. In our secular culture the unwise and the unwary write off forgiveness as something for wimps, do-gooders or fools. But nothing requires more courage than to admit being in the wrong yourself or to forgive those who have wronged you. The easiest thing in life is to harbour anger, resentment or bitterness over both real and imagined slights, injuries, injustices, insults or whatever. The price of extending forgiveness to the party or parties concerned seems too high to pay: a humbling of ourselves, a willingness to understand the one at fault, a compassion towards the "enemy."

What this view overlooks is that withholding forgiveness has its own cost, too. We sometimes think that by withholding forgiveness we're making the other person feel the pain of our hurt. In reality, we're searing our own inner selves with a corrosion that can block the wellspring of our existence. It can radically affect our health for the worse and warp our outlook on the world. Show me a person who is at this moment holding some grudge or brooding over some sense of having been victimized by this or that person or circumstance of life and I'll show you an unhappy man or woman. Forgiveness is not a kind of luxury, then, or something we can do when we decide to get around to it. It needs to be given now – not just for the sake of the one who wronged us but supremely for our own sake. To be quite selfish, forgiving others is in our best interest. It's always a step towards greater wholeness of the body-mind-spirit entity we are.

You may have wondered why, in the Lord's Prayer, it says "forgive us our trespasses (our wrongdoings) as we forgive those who trespass against us." Why is our being forgiven linked so closely to our own forgiving those who have done us wrong? A profound spiritual truth is at stake: we can only really know and accept the fact of forgiveness for ourselves when we experience what it means to forgive others. There are many devout believers in all faiths who have yet to know at any depth what it is to be forgiven by God. The only way to learn that at a gut level is to practise forgiveness ourselves.

Whom should we forgive? First, we need to know what it's like to truly forgive ourselves. It's one thing to examine our own life and conscience, accept blame where it is due and decide to make amends, but it's quite another to indulge in exaggerated or ongoing self-flagellation for past mistakes. That results in misery and saps the energy we need in order to move on. Second, we need to ask ourselves who are the people living or dead who are on our inner "hit list" and forgive them. In some cases, this will mean actually going to the person(s) in question and making things right. In others, it will be enough to show by a changed attitude that forgiveness has been given. Only you really know what or who is screaming out for this kind of action right now in your life.

Finally, many of us need to forgive God. This at first sounds almost blasphemous, but it isn't. The root of bitterness in many people could be dug out if only we could admit that we are angry at God himself. Behind the feeling that our parents, our appearance, education or whatever is responsible for our present unhappiness, there is often a hidden wrath at the Author of life. This has to be brought up to full consciousness, admitted, and dealt with. Aim the anger where it's really directed – at God – and you will find within you the ability to forgive and let your anger go. Nothing you think or say in such an exchange can ever change God's love for you.

THE POWER OF GRATITUDE

There is an old-time evangelical hymn with a great tune called "Count Your Blessings." The title comes from the chorus, which runs:

> Count your blessings, name them one by one.
> Count your blessings, see what God has done.
> Count your blessings, name them one by one;
> And it will surprise you what the Lord has done.

These are very simple words, it's true. But don't be fooled by that. They touch on one of the greatest of all spiritual principles and unlock the secret of enormous spiritual power. Nothing does more for one's overall mental, spiritual and physical health than the careful cultivation of a thankful heart. That is why the Hebrew scriptures, and in particular the Psalms, are so filled with admonitions to give thanks for all the benefits and blessings of this life. The same holds true for the New Testament. It is quite extraordinary, in fact, how often and how eloquently a spiritual genius like St. Paul urges his readers to do everything "with thanksgiving."

But, is it really relevant in our time? I am certain it is. I was reminded of this recently when I was invited to attend a luncheon meeting of the Empire Club of Canada held at the Royal York Hotel in downtown Toronto. The speaker was Sir John Templeton. The large gathering of business people had expected a talk about the economic climate and prospects for investment from the eighty-two-year old multimillionaire. To the surprise of all, he chose instead to speak about the fundamental importance of spiritual values and beliefs today. He began his speech by saying: "We all worry too much. May I suggest we make it a practice to begin each day – no matter what else is going on in our lives – by reminding ourselves of five things for which we can be overwhelmingly grateful." Templeton, who is remarkably fit and strong for his years, said that in his experience nothing was as potent for changing our outlook and transforming the day for the better as this simple yet profound act of gratitude. Of course, just counting one's blessings will not immediately solve a specific problem or ease some pain. But, there is no doubt that the act of remembering how one has been blessed or is being blessed focuses the mind on what God has done and is still doing in our lives. Fresh energy begins to flow and hope is renewed. The fullest spiritual life is the one lived with the most thoroughly thankful mind and soul.

SCIENCE REVISITED

Every one of us wears a pair of invisible spectacles through which we see the world. They colour and shape everything we look at or think about. They are made of those underlying beliefs and assumptions that are at the heart of our present culture. Because they are mostly unconscious, we seldom if ever question them or even acknowledge their existence. The single most important of these is our faith in science and in the scientific method. Unwittingly, as already discussed, we have imbibed the view that science alone "proves" things, that the scientific method is the only one leading to certainty and to true knowledge. It is of paramount importance in our time that while we recognize science's great contributions we remain aware of its limitations. As already noted in the chapter on fuzzy logic, science also lives by faith. The greatest leaps forward are made by the intuitive side of the brain, not the purely rational, reasoning hemisphere. Underlying the scientific enterprise and all scientific advances are the faith assumptions that reason can give us a true picture of reality and that there is order to the cosmos. Science has many areas – in fact lives by this principle – where it is simply agnostic, it just doesn't know, at least not yet. As the eminent physicist Paul Davies says in *The Mind of God*, "There will always be mystery at the end of the universe."

Davies goes on to say, however, that it may be that "there are other forms of understanding which will satisfy the enquiring mind." By this he means the way of faith or of "mysticism." He points out that many notable scientists, such as Einstein, Pauli, Schrödinger, Heisenberg, Eddington, and Jeans, have espoused mysticism. Einstein, for example, spoke of a "cosmic religious feeling" that inspired his reflections on the order and harmony of nature. For Davies, "the scientific method should be pursued as far as it possibly can." But it can only go so far: "I'm not saying that science and logic are likely to provide wrong answers [regarding ultimate questions], but they may be incapable of addressing the sort of 'why' (as opposed to 'how') questions we want to ask."

The great Cambridge astronomer and cosmologist Fred Hoyle spoke for many scientists when he once wrote about a flash of "religious" revelation that revealed to him in an instant the solution to a complex mathematic problem with which he had been wrestling for days. He was driving across some desolate country in northern England on his way to a climbing holiday. Then, "somewhere on Bowes Moor my awareness of the mathematics clarified, not a little, not even a lot, but as if a huge brilliant light had suddenly been switched on." As Davies points out, Hoyle believes that the organization of the universe is controlled by a "superintelligence" who guides its evolution through quantum processes. One could quote a score of others.

At the risk of sounding repetitive, it is really important today, especially for young people, to be on guard against scientism. By this I mean the worship of science in itself and making claims for it that true science itself does not make. One of the strongest deterrents from such a path is knowing that a large number of leading scientists are people of deep religious feeling and belief. Some have been mentioned. Many more could be. But let me just cite one other – Sir Bernard Lovell, who was for many years the leading astronomer at Britain's Jodrell Bank Observatory, and on Sunday a humble lay reader at his parish church.

END TIMES?

As the year 2001, the beginning of the third millennium of this era, draws near, an apocalyptic fervour is starting to manifest itself. Just as happened before the arrival of the year 1001 A.D., everywhere groups are preparing for and predicting the end of the world. I am not a reader of supermarket tabloids but I can't help seeing them while I check out my groceries each week. They are increasingly using screaming headlines about plagues, earthquakes and other signs of the End. A recent one which caught my eye had a picture supposedly of Jesus and under it a huge caption reading, "He will return to earth to battle Satan in 1999." Another front-page story in the same issue predicted "earthquakes and floods will punish the wicked."

In the United States and Canada, especially now with such a vast choice of channels, you can watch preachers on television at almost any hour of the day or night, every day of the week, fulminating about a coming Armageddon, the Rapture of the saved to glory, the return of Christ, and all the rest of the conservative Christian apocalyptic's vision of the future. Sometimes these fundamentalists hold the Bible in one hand and a newspaper in the other as they "prove" that a detailed account of the last days is in scripture and is even now being enacted before our eyes. Even such a widely respected evangelist as Billy Graham is growing more enamoured of these themes as the century draws to a close and he (now seventy-six) grows older. In a more general way, all the churches, by their insistence on a literal interpretation of parts of the New Testament obviously meant to be symbolic, give credence to a similar catastrophic end to world affairs.

No doubt, one day, millions of ages hence, the world as we have known it will be no more. But all this frenzied prophesying, interpreting and predicting of an immediate Return of Christ, the Final Battle between good and evil and so forth, is in my view a lot of nonsense. Yes, there are great risks today – unknown deadly viruses, nuclear blackmail or nuclear war, an environmental collapse, overpopulation, and so on – but none of this is "sent by God" and none of it need vanquish and snuff out the human endeavour. Indeed, the promulgating of pessimistic or catastrophic views about the future is extremely counter-productive. It dampens the will and the imagination we need in order to meet dire challenges. And it makes God out to be some kind of vengeful monster. It also creates a climate for war. The military in the United States, for example, likes to have Christian apocalyptists like the author Hal Lindsey speak at the Pentagon because no group in America is more supportive of defence spending and military preparedness in general than those conservative and fundamentalist Christians who preach that the end of the world is coming.

The other risk, of course, lies in the fringe groups, the religious fanatics who, often arming themselves in the process, are so certain the end is near that they are tempted to provoke it in some way. The Branch Davidian sect, led by David Koresh, and the horrible holocaust which ended its seige at Waco, Texas, or the gassing of commuters on the Tokyo subway by the Japanese religious sect Aum Shinri Kyo, are but two examples of apocalyptic fervour gone very wrong indeed. Unfortunately, there will be more incidents like these in North America and elsewhere before 2001 dawns. It is important for those seeking spiritual growth and enlightenment not to be seduced by any of this end-time propaganda. It is based upon a false

understanding of the Bible and a distorted grasp of
the divine will for our race. It is also based on a fixed
concept of the beginning of time that is, in fact,
unknowable. I have no space to detail all the arguments and the evidence here but, having studied the
texts in detail – including, for example, the obvious
expectation of the author of Revelation that the
events he describes are all to be "quickly" fulfilled – I
can say (and most Christian scholars agree) the Book
of Daniel and the Book of Revelation have nothing
whatever to predict about the details of political and
social life in our time. Those who insist they do are
poor scholars and worse prophets. They are currently
having a field day because many people are fearful as
this century winds down and most lack sufficient
knowledge of the Bible themselves to refute the self-
appointed doomsayers.

It's a widely documented fact that the United
States is the most religious society in the Western
world today. The signs of this are everywhere: presi-
dents and other politicians regularly invoke the
name of God in their speeches; radio and television
in the States devote hours daily to religious program-
ming; the rate of church-going is higher than in any
other major Western country. At the same time, it is
also the most violent.

It's true that the major media have – particularly
since the Jonestown massacre in 1978 and the more
recent events at Waco, Texas – dealt to some extent

with the link between extremist, fringe religious groups and violence. But conservative religion and violence have more in common and a far broader base than anyone I have yet read seems to believe. If you examine closely the religious tenets of a group such as the Branch Davidians or the right-wing militias – or indeed of several racist organizations in the United States and here in Canada as well – you find that they are blatantly "Christian" in rhetoric and ideology.

These groups may take some particular doctrines too far, but the point not to be missed is that for the main part they share a view of the Bible, of God, and hence of human destiny, that is completely mainstream in the States. The God believed in by most Americans (and by many Canadians too) is indistinguishable from the God of David Koresh, of the leaders of the Ku Klux Klan – or, as we no doubt shall see, of Timothy McVeigh, who is in custody and alleged to have been one of the Oklahoma bombers.

Most Americans ultimately worship an extremely violent God. He was asked to bless American violence in Vietnam, in Laos and Cambodia, in Nicaragua and Panama, and most recently (with Billy Graham spending the night at the White House as the bombing began) in the Gulf War. The vision most Americans have that their nation is carrying God's banner in the world and that their "dream" alone has the divine stamp of approval must be understood as the key justification for all acts of violence abroad, whether covert (by the CIA), or overt through the armed forces.

This would be a patent ethical and theological insanity were it not for the nature of the prevailing religious belief. Conservative and fundamentalist Christians, whose religious views are shared by a majority of Americans, believe the Bible is "the Word of God" without qualification. The Bible says an angry God wiped out nearly all humanity with the Flood, commanded the stoning of adulterers and homosexuals, and ordered total genocides – "And David smote the land, and left neither man nor woman alive." And the Bible literalists believe it all. What's more, God, in this view, has prepared a flaming hell in which the bulk of wilful humans will be seared for all eternity.

The truth must be faced squarely. If you believe in and worship a God like that, one who is even now widely believed to be preparing a fiery Apocalypse from which only "saved" Christians will be spared, then violence as a tool of righteousness in the hands of his elect is wholly natural. If it's good enough for your God, then, consciously or unconsciously, it's an option for your community or country. There's an indisputable spiritual law: You become like the object of your devotion. Beliefs shape actions.

Obviously, I'm not saying that all conservative and ultra-conservative Christians are violent. However, it's true that a violent, apocalyptic theology begets a mentality that, under the right circumstances and in certain situations, can beget violent acts. American and Canadian religious leaders, especially those of the conservative camps, need to take a very hard look at what their theology contributes to violence at every level of North American life.

A FINAL WORD ABOUT THE CHURCH

The single most important question to be asked of the Christian Church as we stand at the cusp of the year 2001 is the one asked long ago by the prophet Ezekiel: "Can these dry bones come alive again?"

Perhaps you remember the story, which is told in Ezekiel 37. The prophet had a vision in which he found himself looking over the scene of an ancient battlefield. The bones of the dead lay scattered around. In the New Revised Standard Version of the Bible (in my view, the best translation available today), the text reads: "Mortal, can these bones live? I answered, O Lord God, you know. Then he said to me, Prophesy to these bones, and say to them: 'O dry bones, hear the word of the Lord. Thus says the Lord God to these bones: I will cause breath to enter you, and you shall live. I will lay sinews on you, and will cause flesh to come upon you, and cover you with skin, and put breath in you, and you shall live; and you shall know that I am the Lord.' So I prophesied as

I had been commanded; and as I prophesied, suddenly there was a noise, a rattling, and the bones came together, bone to its bone."

As the old spiritual song so graphically portrays it, the visionary miracle happened. The bones came together – "the hip bone connected to the thigh bone. . . ." They were clad with skin, but there was still no breath in them. Then Ezekiel is told to prophesy to the wind (spirit) to breathe upon the slain that they might live. He says: "I prophesied as he commanded me, and the breath came into them, and they lived, and stood on their feet, a vast multitude." The prophet is then told that this company represents the whole "house of Israel" and that God is about to raise up his people just as the dead in the vision have been raised. "I will put my Spirit within you," he promises.

Today, the churches resemble the valley of dry bones. People want spiritual bread and the breath of life as never before, but instead they are given meaningless rituals and limiting, enslaving dogmas. Sermons lack relevance, passion and sustenance for mind or spirit. Scripture lessons tell us about distant people who knew the reality of God in their lives, but they are often impenetrable for us today because of their obscure references to places and tribes completely alien to our own experience. It all tends to remind one of a vast, archeological dig. On all sides, tradition takes precedence over compassion and honesty. An obsession with the past for its own sake prevents the church from facilitating a breakthrough of the divine Spirit to meet the needs of today. The Anglican Church, which is in great crisis, loves to sing: "As it was in the beginning, is now and ever shall be. Amen." But, in many ways, this is the motto for all religion. Everywhere people are searching for God and instead are offered hoary, virtually incomprehensible creeds with the hand of death upon them.

Here and there, the warmth of like-minded souls gathered together creates a kind of fellowship. But increasingly these congregations resemble shrinking clubs or enclaves destined to come under the Ministry for Multiculturalism or some other agency for the promotion of anachronistic ways. Elsewhere, among the fundamentalists, there is the appearance of life as one small segment of society capitulates to the siren call of simplistic or absolutist answers to life's complexities. But these ultra-conservative denominations, in spite of their apparent vigour in some quarters, are in just as much trouble as their more liberal counterparts. They are in for a big shock when all their carefully honed answers finally crumble before the onslaught of ever-increasing knowledge. Already straining the bounds of credibility, their doctrines will prove unable to answer the intellectual call of more and more of their adherents.

What, then, is the answer? For me it's clear, and we don't need a new religion to find it. If the spiritual principles lived and taught by Jesus had been the central focus of the Church's teaching all down the ages, we would not be in the mess we are in today. I repeat what I first said in *For Christ's Sake*: "Jesus is not only the greatest person who ever lived, he is also the most misunderstood." Instead of plumbing the implications of what he said and how he lived, the Church has rivetted attention on his person. So much so, in fact, that by a tragic paradox Jesus as currently proclaimed has become a block to people finding God! As we have seen earlier, Jesus never taught a creed; he lived and taught life itself. His basic axiom was that the sense of God's power, presence and love that he intimately experienced was open to all. He had discovered his true nature as a child of God and hence of the universe. This awareness of being part of "the Kingdom of God" and the knowledge that God dwells in every person – "the Kingdom of heaven is within you" – combined to produce his radical ethic of forgiveness and justice for all. He predicted that when this message was accepted and lived a fresh outpouring of God's Spirit would energize humanity. Until the Church rediscovers all of this, unfortunately it is little more than a collection of dry bones.

Where Is God?

Where is God to be found? Today, scientists like Paul Davies find him indirectly through the evidence of an awesome design and order in the origins and evolution of the cosmos. Indeed the natural world has been the source of religious wonder and experience for our species from earliest times. As the Psalmist put it some 2,500 years ago: "The heavens declare the glory of God and the firmament showeth His handiwork." Human beings of every tribe and culture in every region of the earth have from the very dawn of self-aware consciousness stood in reverent amazement at the Mind, Energy or Presence behind and in and through all things. They have called this numinous mystery by a thousand different names but the message has been essentially one: God makes himself known to us through the movement of the stars, the flow of the seasons, the rivers and oceans and through all living things. It is not surprising that most people, whether religious or unchurched, feel closer to God out under the starry sky, by a waterfall, or on a mountaintop than in any sacred building or at any formal ritual. God is in nature; or, more properly, nature itself is in God. We meet him there, as I said at the very outset.

But, as I also pointed out, we meet God in one another too. So often on my travels or in my ordinary day-to-day living I have encountered – usually totally out of the blue – someone in whose face there is a kind of special light or shining quality as if the sacred Presence within were illumining the whole personality. It was not just a matter of the glow of animal health because frequently the person concerned was ill or disadvantaged in some way, or even dying. But I could sense between myself and the other person Another One. It has often happened with small groups of people, as well. If, as I have argued, we are designed as spiritual beings, then whenever there is a meeting of minds and hearts in a relationship or in a common cause for good, God is to be found in our midst. We need to celebrate this much more than we do.

We can find God again and again in the events of our lives, especially once we are consciously committed to seeking to know and do his will, just as the Jewish authors of the Hebrew Bible were certain they saw him working in their history of liberation. The authors of the Torah – the first five Books of Moses – believed they found and came to know God through the Law. The great prophets of Israel saw and knew him in ethical principles and, above all, deeds of justice and mercy, especially towards the poor and the oppressed. So, too, we can find God in the promptings of our conscience and in our awareness of a moral law within us. We can find him in acts of compassion and generosity towards all, particularly those in great need.

As one who struggles to follow Christ as a disciple, though not as a worshipper, I have to state that for me he is the person in whom God has shown his most human face. It is in him that the God of nature and the God of utterly unfathomable mystery becomes focused in such a way that I see his mercy and forgiveness and love towards all most clearly. I do not believe Jesus was God in any sense that is not open to every one of us. But, although I have learned so very much from other teachers, leaders, and faiths, I personally find that it is in Jesus that I catch the fullest glimpse of the humanity of God. He was totally open to and filled with God's Spirit, a fully realized human being. I see God in the words and life of Jesus as I see him nowhere else – the loving father on the road running to meet and embrace his son who was rebellious and lost. We are all that prodigal child, Christians and non-Christians alike.

Finally, though, we must find God much closer to hand than atop a mountain or beside the ocean or in a temple if we are to find what Jesus discovered for himself. What he found, and what constitutes the single most important truth this book contains, is that the God of the universe is within us. Ultimately, we do not have to run to this or that guru or to this or that special meeting; we do not have to range the world seeking a revelation. God's presence or Spirit – "the light which lighteneth every person who comes into the world" – is closer to you than your own breathing, nearer than hands or feet. You can call this presence "the Christ" or "the Christ Mind" or the Atman, or simply "the Spirit." The founder of the Quakers, George Fox, called it "that of God within," as well as "the inner light." You and I, as St. Paul once reminded his readers, are the "tabernacles" or dwelling place of God. As I said earlier, we hold this great treasure in ourselves. Seek out that Presence in your own stillness. Look for it in others. Hold to it above all other dogmas and rituals however important they may be for you. Then you will have a faith for yourself and for your children not just for 2001 but for the wider, glorious future God is calling us and all humanity to share. And you don't have to deny your intellect to do this.

We are presently, in spite of all the enormous problems facing humanity, in the midst of a vast, worldwide spiritual awakening. God's call to each of us is to become a vital part of that. As you decide what your own response must be, I want to leave with you two brief statements from the Hebrew Bible which continue to give me insight and fresh strength for the journey. One is a promise. The other is a challenge. Both are given from the New Revised Standard Version. First the promise: "Be strong and courageous; do not be frightened or dismayed, for the Lord your God is with you wherever you go." (Joshua 1:9). Then the challenge: "What does the Lord require of you but to do justice, and to love kindness, and to walk humbly with your God?" (Micah 6:8). So be it.